A History of the
Music and Musicians
of S. Chad's, Shrewsbury

David Leeke

FOREWORD

The Vicar and Rural Dean of Shrewsbury,
The Reverend Prebendary Mark W Thomas

I remember clearly being shown round S. Chad's by the then Bishop of Shrewsbury in 2000, before being appointed Vicar. The High School choir were rehearsing for a concert, and I immediately realised what a wonderful space for music this extraordinary building provided. From the outset of my ministry here I wanted S. Chad's to be a church where the music that was offered was both excellent and inclusive, to the glory of God, for the building up of his Church and for the enrichment of the life of the town.

David Leeke has been the ideal director of music to help us realise that vision. He knows that music is an essential part of our mission. His passion for music and his love for Shrewsbury and for S. Chad's have seen a wonderful revival of music of all sorts in the church in the years since his appointment, and we are doubly blessed that he has been joined by Richard Walker as his deputy. So I am delighted to commend this book by David about the story of S. Chad's music. It reveals a distinguished history, and is well-timed to celebrate the magnificent Harrison and Harrison rebuild of our organ. The relationship between Incumbent and Director of Music can occasionally be a fraught one, but it is very good to have on record that at S. Chad's that relationship seems to have worked for the benefit of both church and community.

Mark Thomas.

A History of the Music and Musicians
of S. Chad's, Shrewsbury

by David Leeke

ISBN 978-0-9572501-0-9

Published by S. Chad's, Shrewsbury

S. Chad's Terrace, Shrewsbury SY1 1JX

Artwork by MA Creative, Shrewsbury
www.macreative.co.uk
Cover photos by Mike Ashton

ACKNOWLEDGEMENTS

The publication of this book would not have been possible without the help and support of many people.

I am immensely grateful to our Vicar, Mark Thomas, for his introductory words. The musical life of S. Chad's and the account of it as revealed in this book are the result of the efforts of more than one person.

My predecessor but one, Bill Smallman has been extraordinarily helpful by supplying some of the historical data, much of it researched at the time of the organ's centenary in 2004.

Dr Roy Massey, for many years Organist of Hereford Cathedral, and a former President of The Royal College of Organists, has long been a good friend to S. Chad's, most recently in giving the inaugural recital of the restored organ in January 2012. He was so delighted with the work by Harrison and Harrison, that he too has undertaken some research; specifically into the pedigree of the organ, in order to write a substantial article for national and international periodicals about this fine instrument.

Janice Brown has undertaken a colossal amount of research and the painstaking gathering of snippets of information on all aspects of the musical life of S. Chad's over the centuries. She has culled her information from numerous sources and I am particularly grateful to her for this detailed labour of love. Without her efforts, much of the information contained here could never have been written.

I am very grateful to Richard and Gay Walker for proof reading the final document, and to Kathryn Burningham for her encouragement and patient work in correcting numerous proofs.

David Leeke
April 2012

Part 1 –
MUSICAL HISTORY

The Old Church

Information about the musical life of S. Chad's is rather scanty; much of it seems to lack documentation or is confused and contradictory. S. Chad's is the oldest Christian foundation in the town, dating from the eighth century, and it certainly seems that Old S. Chad's, with its College of Canons, enjoyed prestigious music, although the precise details are vague. What is widely documented is that the County Architect, a young Thomas Telford, informed the S. Chad's officials that the church was in a dangerous state; they failed to respond to this information, and the building collapsed in the early hours of 9 July 1788.

It seems that in the months leading up to this calamity the organ had been renovated and repaired, although little information exists as to the details of this instrument or the nature and extent of the repair. Some sources state that a three-manual instrument built by Harris and Byfield was in the old church, but this is hard to substantiate. Dr W L Sumner in his book *The Organ* refers to an instrument being built for the church in 1716 by Thomas Schwarbrook (or Schwarbrick or Swarbrick); however Sumner suggests that this was removed in 1794. As by that date the new church had already been built, this is clearly not entirely accurate. Although little remained of the original building or its contents, there is an account which suggests that wrecked pipes from the church organ were found in the ruins, possibly as well as an organ case which was regarded as being by Harris and Byfield.

This may well be the organ case which is now in S. Mary's Church. However, a report by John Norman on the organ in S. Mary's in the last quarter of the twentieth century suggests that this case may be by Swarbrick because of its similarity with the known Swarbrick case in S. Philip's Cathedral, Birmingham. During the years it took to build the new church, the congregation of S. Chad's worshipped at S. Mary's. Therefore it is feasible that this church received as a gift the rescued S. Chad's organ case. Certainly the famous Jesse window at the east end of S. Mary's was also originally in Old S. Chad's, and, when recovered from the ruins, was presented to S. Mary's as a gift for their hospitality during the years S. Chad's was without a church. Apparently the original S. Chad's organ case was capped with a statue of S. Chad which was also removed from the ruins, but it is unclear what has happened to this in the intervening years. It seems that these two great Collegiate Churches shared the same organist for much of the eighteenth century, as will be seen in the biographical details of post holders below. It was only after the building of the new S. Chad's that the two churches had separate musicians on their staff.

After much controversy which is well-documented elsewhere (and is beyond the scope of this particular book), the new church was completed in 1792 occupying a commanding position on a hill overlooking the Quarry. A new three-manual instrument was installed at a cost of four hundred guineas by the father and son firm of Robert and William Gray; the specification of this instrument can be found in Appendix 1. It was not a large instrument and stood back from the gallery balcony. In her book *New S. Chad's and its Architect,* Mary Hill suggests that this was considered a fine instrument at the time. Yet in the same book she contradicts this, stating that it gave a good deal of trouble in its first three years of use! It is uncertain what was used to accompany the services from 23 August 1792 (the date on which the new church was dedicated and opened for worship) until 1794 when the new instrument was installed. The *Salopian Journal* of 1794 reports that the year started with a *"deep fall of snow and tremendous gusts of wind which occasioned very considerable damage"* (29 January); that our armies fought on the Rhine and Moselle, and in Flanders and the Netherlands; that Lord Clive (HM Lord Lieutenant for Shropshire) proposed augmentation of the county militia for the internal defence of the kingdom; and that, late in the year, there were fireworks to celebrate the *'Glorious Victory at Sea'* over the French. In addition, during the summer, reports of Englishmen guillotined in France can be seen among accounts of the *"long continuance of dry weather"* which had *"been fatal to peas and damaged beans".* However, it is also noted that wheat and hops had never been *"more promising".*

The interior of the church was redecorated in 1814-1816 and this included *"crimson moreen curtains with 40 yards of crimson lace"* for the back of the organ. The new church had always been very dark inside after sunset as it was lit only by a strictly limited number of candles in 12 holders; candle branches were not even placed on the pulpit. The need for more artificial light became urgent when evensong was taken at night instead of in the afternoon. So three chandeliers were bought *"for better lighting the church"* in 1819, but it was to be several more years before the thrifty trustees allowed candles for the use of the singers *"when practising".* Members of the choir had received salaries (paid out of rates) for many years, and in 1825 a *"professional person to assist in leading the singers and attend to their behaviour in church"* was engaged at a salary of £10 p.a. Who this person was is not known. However, this could have been necessary as the Organist at the time, John Wynne, was blind, and perhaps this precluded him from carrying out such duties. In 1829, it was resolved that an extra £10 yearly be placed in the hands of the Vicar and Curate *"to ensure a permanent and better choir";* also that year, the royal arms in the church gallery were shifted to make room for *"a more convenient seat for the singers".*

In the 1840s improvements costing £80 were made to the organ, and the choir seats were again extended. The trustees were understandably unhappy to be told in 1841 that the singers' salaries should not be paid out of rates. As the church had no income apart from Church Rate and pew rents (often in arrears) the trustees' first reaction was *"that unless the Singers can be paid out of the Rates, they must be altogether abandoned which would be a great inconvenience to the service of the Church".*

John Wynne was Organist of S. Chad's for nearly 62 years, resigning in April 1846 with the following letter addressed to the churchwardens of the parish:

Shrewsbury
27 April 1846

Gentlemen,

I beg to inform you that I have this day resigned into the hands of the Mayor and Corporation from whom I received it, the appointment of Organist to the Parish Church of St Chad.

I remain,
Gentlemen,
Your obedient servant
John Wynne

(Shropshire Archives 1048/829)

Attached to the letter is a note:

Received this notice at ¼ past 2pm 27 April 1846. Shewed it to Mr Edward Hughes and Mr John Lloyd at ½ past 7pm the same day. Shewed it to Mr Thomas Jobson at ½ past 8pm the same day.

Within a few weeks of this resignation there were lengthy legal discussions and correspondence about exactly who had, or should have, the right of appointment of the new Organist. The reference numbers refer to documents which can be viewed in the Shropshire Archives:

"...First, whether the appointment of organist at the Parish Church of St. Chad can still be legally as heretofore be made by the Corporation or, if not whether the arrangement that has now subsisted for upwards of a Century ought not to be put an end to by other parties and the arrangements namely the Parishioners at large or whether you consider that the right of appointment is needed by the Act for rebuilding the Church in the Trustees will be in the Minister and Churchwardens for the time being under clause pages 18 and 19.

"Secondly, whether you consider that under the provisions of the Municipal Corporation Act the Corporation can any longer legally pay a salary to the Organist of St. Chad and if you are of opinion that they are bound to do so in case the arrangement with the Parish as to the appointment is departed from.

"I am of the opinion that the appointment of Organist ought no longer to be made by the Corporation. It does not appear to me that the act for rebuilding the church has vested

the right of appointment in the Trustees. The reason why they are empowered to set up an Organ under the 22nd Section is because there was an Organ in the Old Church at the time of its destruction which appears to have been placed there by the parish." (1048/830)

"I am clearly of opinion that an Organist is not a person contemplated by the 10th section to be 'necessary and proper for the purposes of the Act' and that even if the trust funds may be applied to the payment of an Organist under the 33rd section as included within the term 'Servants' (of which I entertain some doubt) these two sections will not have the effect of giving the power of appointing the Organist to the Trustees. As the parishioners must eventually provide for the payment of the Organist's salary, I think the right of appointment must be in them." – Fred Thesiger, Temple, 28 July 1846

"Note: When the parishioners cease to provide the funds by the abolition of Church Rate in the Parish the pewholders who fund the money must also elect their own organist". (1048/831)

"By direction of the council of this Borough…to forward you for the information of yourself and the other Parochial authorities of St. Chad a copy of the opinion of Mr Fred Thesiger upon the case stated on behalf of the Corporation with reference to the appointment and salary of the organist of St. Chad." (1048/831)

The wrangling continued and a summary of this case was made on 21 August 1846 *"for the opinion of Mr Prideaux"* (Town Clerk) stating that the corporation had appointed Mr Baker in 1716, and *"on his death* [incorrect] *had appointed Mr James Burney who continued until 1785 when they appointed Mr Wynne…In 1788, the organ and bells were entirely destroyed…In 1792, the new organ was bought by the Trustees…Prior to 1803, it does not appear any salary was paid by the Trustees to the Organist…Mr Wynne's salary had increased to £25 in 1803, and the corporation had paid for repairs… Mr Wynne has resigned and a new person elected by the Corporation to fill the place at £25, but the Trustees have elected another gentleman! This is the first vacancy since the Act."*

Further documents exist detailing the case of those for and against the method by which the new Organist was appointed. There is also a document stating the need for a 'Queen's Advocate'. A Mr Vaughan Williams stated that the appointment was *"in the right of the parishioners, not the Vicar"* which has a particular interest to musicians.

Shrewsbury's most famous son, Charles Darwin, was baptised in the church in November 1809 and attended S. Chad's with his mother Susannah as a young boy. He was related to the Wedgwood family, as was the composer Ralph Vaughan Williams. It might therefore be possible that Mr Vaughan Williams (mentioned here) was related to the Darwins of Shrewsbury and thus to the famous composer, but this cannot be proved. More significantly, after all this extensive legal debate, the name of Wynne's successor has proved impossible to track down!

What is known is that major repairs to the organ took place in 1848, perhaps at the insistence of the new post holder. Gray and Davison submitted an estimate on 8 December 1847 for work which included putting in a pair of horizontal bellows and some valves to prevent tremors in the wind supply. The organ was cleaned and some tonal improvements made and it was enlarged to contain 27 speaking stops. A Clarabella replaced a Mounted Cornet stop ("*a totally useless stop*" – sic!) and the cost was £236 with an additional cost of £60 to make a "new swell similar to S. Mary's". Gray and Davison stated that "*the general [organ] fabric is in perfectly sound and durable condition, highly likely to remain for a century*". Repairs were also made to the "*gilt front speaking pipes*", and it was also commented that "*the organ was last cleaned by Mr Gray 24 years ago*" (1823-4 when it seems pedals were added) and that "*the front pipes might have been preserved had attention been directed to them in proper time*". At the same time, a "*Bourden*" (sic) stop "*was placed in the Choir organ to meet the Double in the Swell*" at a cost of £12.

By 1851 the edition of the *Directory for Shropshire* includes the following under the entry for S. Chad's: "*Over the chief entrance is a powerful and fine-toned organ, built by Gray, of London, in 1794, and enlarged and improved in 1848.*"

The first mention of any children in the choir was in 1850, when the Organist was told to spend an hour a week instructing a group of children from S. Chad's School in church music; the children did not receive 'salaries' but 'merit money'. It seems that at this time a custom (still in existence in the 1960s) developed of initiating new choirboys by throwing them over the top of the Quarry wall and then dousing them under the conduit at the top of Claremont Bank!

In 1856 the trustees told the Bishop and Vicar that the church was not the right place for performances of oratorios, even if the aim of the concerts was to raise money for the Charity Schools.

"*There is a strong feeling of objection in the minds of many of the Parishioners, and the Trustees do not think after the large expenditure in decorating and improving the Church it is expedient to permit any use of the sacred building that may injure its improved Condition*".

Despite its glowing description in the 1851 Directory, the organ continued to give concern. Mary Hill's book suggests that a '*new*' organ was given in 1861 by Colonel G E Wingfield, CC, although it is more likely that this was yet another rebuild or restoration of the existing organ, again undertaken by Gray and Davison. In fact, Gray and Davison were at that time Shrewsbury's favourite organ builders; in addition to S. Chad's they had instruments in S. Mary's, S. Alkmund's, The Abbey, S. Giles, S. George's and S. Michael's!

An invoice in the Shropshire Archives (1048/626) dated 18 July 1861 itemises the extras involved in its installation, which included:

	s d	
"Altering benches in gallery	4 / 4½	
Making umberella (sic) guard and tin	2 / - *	*(*this has been marked 'less!')*
Nails, screws and glew (sic)	1 / 3	

as well as *"Curtains (red dale), Fixing spring to door, Labour (self & boy), Framing for organ seat, Brass buttons & screws, Painting above pipe and casing round door".*

There must have been a surfeit of keyboard instruments in the church in the 1860s, as another invoice (1048/5159) in 1864 shows a cost of £14-11s-11d for the *"harmonium"*. That invoice also shows a charge for *"music repairing"* (£6-4s-1d), while another (1048/5178) itemises the music purchases for the choir from 'J B Boucher & Co - Music and Musical Instrument Sellers':

"September:	*3 Hymns Ancient & Modern @ 1/6*
	3 Psalters @ 2/6
October:	*4 Psalters @ 2/6*
	12 Canticles @ 1/6
	3 Hymns FF @ ½d
November:	*6 Chants @ 6d*
	2 Hymn Books @ 1/6"

It is unfortunate that the holder of the post of Organist in these exciting times is unnamed.

1865-1884

Certainly by January 1865 (and perhaps earlier) the post was held by Walter Cecil Hay, who, by all accounts, was a fine musician. He submitted details as outlined in Shropshire Archives (1048/5166) of the cash paid to the choirboys at Christmas 1864. Records of these payments exist for many years following, and include *"half a year's salary (minus fines) due at Midsummer 1866"* to eight boys (but sadly none to the ninth, a certain Master Williams whose 'merit money' had been completely cancelled out by fines!) The choir was obviously singing regular anthems at this time as Hay submitted an invoice in the summer of 1865 showing anthems purchased:

"February: 18 'Behold how good' @ 1½d
May: 8 treble pt 'Lift up' @ 1½d
June: 4 bass, 4 tenor, 2 alto @ 1½d"

There is also another invoice (1048/5180) from 1865 relating to the 'harmonium', this one specifically *"to repairing"* on Lady Day. At Christmas 1866, there is an invoice (1048/5182) for more work done to the harmonium at a cost of 6 shillings. It is repaired again (only 4 shillings this time) the following year, and in addition at Christmas 1867 there is a further invoice for *"4 new notes and tuning of the harmonium"*.

The importance of the choir at this time is further substantiated by purchases in 1866 to 1868, which included *"5 Lichfield Psalters, 7 Cheadle Chant Books, 7 Canticles (2d), 3 Tallis Responses (3d), 5 Hymns A & M (1/2), Psalter & Canticles (2/8), Responses (3d), 12 copies of 'Brightest and Best' (@ ½d), and 10 copies of 'How Beautiful' (@ 1½d)"*.   (Shropshire Archives references: 1048/5181 and 1048/5185)

Interestingly, there is also a receipt (1048/5176) dated 4 May 1868: *"Received from the Rev. Yardley [Vicar] as Treasurer, the Sum of Two Guineas for the Rent of Two Pews occupied by St. Chad's Choir"*.

Mary Hill states that *"the building debt was paid off at last in 1867, and in 1870 the trustees' powers under the building acts came to an end. They wished to hand it over in good condition and were faced by a report which, after saying that 'the Church, looking upon it as a sacred edifice, is very far from being in a creditable state', went on to catalogue minor and major defects...The trustees did their best, undeterred by a legal opinion that nearly everything they had done in the past 40 years had been 'ultra vires'"* Looking over the various archival documents, one can see several instances of their exceeding the scope of their powers!

It is not absolutely certain when adult singers ceased to receive remuneration for their services, but what is certain is that a *"Voluntary and Robed Choir"* was established in the summer of 1877. One of the church clergy was given a specific role in relation to the choir and the church's worship, and was given the title of Precentor. This is essentially the founding of the choir as it still is today.

A set of rules dated 1 July 1877 were drawn up as follows:

'RULES OF S. CHAD'S VOLUNTARY CHOIR'

"This choir shall be called 'S. Chad's Voluntary Choir'"

This choir shall be composed exclusively of men and boys and will be managed by a Precentor, Choirmaster, the Churchwardens for the time being and Committee of Seven which committee shall be chosen annually.

One of the Committee shall be appointed annually to act as Registrar, whose duty it shall be to keep a correct Register of the punctual attendances of the Members of the Choir, both at Services and at Practices: and to conduct any correspondence that may be necessary in reference thereto.

That Members shall consider themselves to be under the control of the Precentor, and in the case of a disagreement arising, the matter shall be referred to him, and his decision (subject to the approval of the Vicar) shall be final.

Any one wishing to join the Choir shall apply to the Registrar, and having obtained his permission to attend practices, shall do so for one month, at the end of which period if the Precentor accedes to admit him, he, by signing a copy of these Rules, shall become a Member; and in case of his wishing to leave the Choir, he must signify his intention of so doing to the Registrar one month previously.

The Committee shall have power to expel a Member for misbehaviour.

Two practices shall be held weekly, at one of which each Member must attend, or pay a fine not exceeding three-pence for an Adult and one half-penny for a Juvenile, unless he receives permission to be absent from the Registrar; also each Member must give notice to the Registrar at one of the practices, which services he intends to be present at on the following Sunday, (everyone is expected to attend two), and failing to keep his promise shall be fined a sum not exceeding six pence for an Adult and one penny for a Juvenile; and all fines shall be fixed by the Precentor, paid to the Registrar, and be disposed of as the Committee think fit.

All Notices shall be posted in the Choir Vestry by the Registrar on a board provided for that purpose.

None of the foregoing Rules shall be altered, and no fresh one shall be added except at a General Meeting of the Members of the Choir, and unless the alteration or addition shall be agreeable to the Clergy, Churchwardens and Choirmaster for the time being."

The Voluntary Choir's Minute Books (two of Committee Meetings 1877-1897 and another of General Meetings 1877-1884) are fortunately still in existence and make fascinating reading. Oddly, the Organist was not involved with the administration or running of the Choir in any way, so was not a member of the Committee, though the Vicar, Mr Yardley, did suggest that Mr Hay should meet them 'periodically'.

The Committee not only monitored attendance (those not complying with the Rules being *"requested not to attend again"*), but also approved the admittance of new members to the choir. The members were also heavily involved in the maintenance of good behaviour, holding Courts *"to enquire into the conduct of certain boy members of the choir"* (including investigating the injury sustained by one boy after being dropped over the wall of S. Chad's Terrace, as well as one particular incident whose record covers several pages in the Minute Book for 1880); suspensions and expulsions were not uncommon. The planning of the annual Choir Treat, managing the funds, and ordering Psalters, Hymn Books, Chant Books and robes, as well as arranging pigeon holes to store the music and cupboards for surplices, also came under the Committee's jurisdiction.

The General Meeting of 29 June 1877 records that *"Some conversation ensued as to the appointment of a Choirmaster in addition to the Organist. The Churchwardens present said that they could give no definite answer at the present time as the Senior Warden was absent at the seaside, but they would have a Meeting to which they would summon Mr Hay and would inform the Registrar as to their decision. Several other matters [not recorded] were also mentioned to the Churchwardens which they promised to communicate to the Organist."*

A year later *"The subject as to a Choir Master was referred to the Annual General Meeting"*, and at that AGM (held on 4 July 1878), *"Some discussion ensued as to the necessity of appointing a Choirmaster in addition to the Organist."* But the Senior Warden *"informed the Meeting that the matter had not been lost sight of since the last Annual General Meeting and that he was at present in communication with the Organist and he could assure them that the matter should be looked into"*.

It seems that the matter <u>was</u> looked into, as a month later (12 August) there is the first mention in the Minutes of a Mr Penn in connection not only with the annual treat which was to be held on Monday 26th August *"provided that Mr Penn could go then"* but also regarding the Precentor who would *"provide for the Practices in the absence of Mr Penn"*. At the following month's meeting, it was recorded that Mr Penn was to *"rearrange the Sides of the Choir"* and also *"arrange music for the Infirmary Meeting"*.

Christopher Penn, a Solicitor's Managing Clerk by profession, was in his mid-thirties when appointed as Choirmaster at S. Chad's. Born in Northamptonshire to Edward Penn (a gardener and sexton) and a mother who died within just a few years of his birth, Christopher had married Elizabeth Hilditch Macartney (a schoolmistress from Chatham, Kent) on 5 July 1870 at Holy Cross Church, Shrewsbury (Shrewsbury Abbey); by 1878 they already had four children, and, over the next ten years, went on to have five more.

At a meeting on 17 February 1879, the Librarian *"complained of the way in which the Books were treated by Members of the Choir; it was agreed that the Bags should again be used"*; it was also decided that some Manuscript Books should be ordered, and that *"a representation be made to the Churchwardens as to the insufficiency of the Light in the Vestry"*. At the following meeting, *"a long discussion ensued as to what had better be done as to several of the members of the Choir who were useless"* and *"it was decided that there should be a trial of voices of members of the Choir periodically"*, the first to take place before the practice on 24 March.

A new Rule (proposed by a Mr Cross) was discussed later that month:

> *"That in event of a boy's voice breaking, he having been a member of the Choir for two years previous he shall be entitled to election as honorary member of the Choir. And he shall be so elected if upon the representation of the clerical superintendent, registrar and Choirmaster for the time being his behaviour, attendance and general conduct has been deemed satisfactory. Honorary members thus elected will be required to sit in seats allocated to them in Church to occupy the same before the Clergy and Choir enter, to join in the responses, and (as presumably they will be older than the ordinary boy members of the Choir) to set an example of godly reverence in the House of God. It shall also be the duty of the Registrar to keep account of their attendance and behaviour and in event of the same being satisfactory honorary members shall be entitled to participate in any annual treat or club sports of the Choir or any extra benefit provided by private hands for the benefit of the Choir provided that the donor of such gift and the Committee of the Choir deem it advisable to include them. And in event of the attendance and conduct of honorary members being unsatisfactory it shall be the duty of the registrar to report the same to the committee of the Choir who shall and are hereby invested with power to punish either by suspension of the privileges or by deprivation of honorary membership the boy complained of ".*

The choir gave a concert in April at S. Chad's Girls' Schoolroom (which was the Committee's second choice of venue - the Working Men's Club rules did not permit a concert by the Church Choir to be given in their hall), and the profits were put towards the annual Treat.

In June, Mr Cross said that he had another new rule *"relating to the Voices"* to propose, but would leave it until Mr Penn was ready with his report.

The Committee Report for the 1879 AGM included the following comment: *"Your Committee are also pleased to report that thanks to the untiring energy and able direction of Mr Penn, for which they feel themselves unable to express to any adequate extent their sense of deep gratitude they have severally been complimented from various quarters upon the efficiency of the Choir during the past year."*

The following month it was agreed that *"steps be taken at once to provide every member of the choir with a chant book"* and also that several anthems and a set of King's Evening Service be purchased.

On Tuesday 9 September, at 3.00pm the choir gave their services at the ceremony of the laying of the Foundation Stone at the Eye & Ear Hospital (now apartments known as Kingsland Bridge Mansions).

A sub-committee met next to "take into consideration the conduct of several boys", two of them for "general bad conduct" (they lost 3 months' merit money as a result and were also "warned as to their future behaviour") and a further six for "inattention" (they were "severely lectured"). Sadly, two of the older boys were also summoned to the next meeting to be thanked for their services and asked to resign as their voices were "now of no service".

Three people (one man and two boys) were admitted in November, but one boy, whose conduct was unsatisfactory, was not admitted. Mr Penn was also instructed to speak to one Choirman "as to his non-attendance" He then announced that a friend of Mr Hay had generously offered to give to the 'best boys' four handsomely bound oratorios and several money prizes; the offer was accepted, though it was later felt that the donor should be made aware that among the junior members recently "there had been a much greater exhibition of zeal than efficiency"! (Maybe this is the explanation for a resolution a month later that "no boy be allowed in church before Service".)

1880 started with a report that Mr Hay was anxious for the Choir to take part in the Choral Festival to be held in Lichfield Cathedral on 10 June, suggesting that, as the expenses would be great, this could replace the annual Treat; however, the committee felt it necessary to ascertain the financial position before making any decision on that. The Vicar donated a sum of money to enable the Choir to join the Lichfield Diocesan Choral Association, and it was agreed that the music for the Festival should be purchased as soon as possible. It appears that it was later decided that ("owing to the shortness of time available for practising") the Choir would "defer until the next opportunity" when it would be able to take a more active part in the proceedings.

The Report of the Committee, printed for the AGM in July, states that all proceedings connected with the Choir had been duly chronicled in the Parish Magazine, and goes on to thank Mr Penn for "his valuable services as choirmaster, as well as for the uniform kindness and sympathy which have endeared him to every member of the Choir. Your committee feel their inability to express, to a sufficient extent, their thanks, and the feeling is universal that long as he remains to superintend their efforts the welfare of the Choir is assured". The [Voluntary] Choir having now been in existence for three years, it was felt that the Committee no longer needed to meet every month; this decision is borne out by the noticeable intervals between meetings thereafter.

In November, "a case of misbehaviour" was reported by "certain inhabitants of St John's Hill"; this matter was taken very seriously and the case is recorded in great detail. Six boys were charged but "two of them strongly denied any complicity therein and, no evidence to incriminate them being forthcoming, the case against them fell through"; however, two of the others "having confessed to taking part in the misbehaviour were left to have such punishment meted out to them as could be warranted after the whole case was heard". The easiest way to summarise this is to quote the letter of effusive apology which was signed by the four boys found guilty at the Court: "We the undersigned members of St Chad's Choir do *beg to tender our apologies to Mr & Mrs P----- (and Mr & Mrs F-----) of St John's Hill, Shrewsbury, for that we have on various occasion, when returning from choir practice, annoyed them by pushing open their door, and we beg to assure them that we will for the future not only abstain ourselves from like conduct, but will use every means in our power to prevent others committing it either in our presence or by our privy consent, and we trust that in overlooking our past misbehaviour Mr & Mrs P----- (and Mr & Mrs F-----) will believe us when we assert that we have never upon any occasion acted towards themselves in a spirit of special ill-will, but have amused ourselves thoughtlessly and in disregard of the feelings of others generally to whom our conduct has been a source of annoyance."* The boys were taken down to Mr P----- and Mr F----- to tender their apologies for their past misconduct which were accepted. Incidentally, although the two boys who had voluntarily confessed their own misconduct received a special caution not to repeat the offence they had no marks deducted from them, the other two miscreants had 100 and 80 marks respectively deducted from their total at the end of the quarter.

Mr Penn announced later that month that the choir concert might be got ready by the latter end of January 1881; at that same meeting, there was discussion about the feasibility of the choir's being involved in the Lichfield Mission service, and three gentlemen accepted the post of collectors on behalf of the choir to co-operate with those appointed by the Temperance Society and the School Committee in assisting with the purchase of the Parish pianoforte. Several members had remarked that *"the kneeling down was not properly attended to"* and it was *"carried unanimously that all members be particularly requested to kneel down while the prayers are being said"*.

On Advent Sunday (1880), the Vicar said that the choir should be surpliced at all services, a change welcomed by all members; an extra official had been elected to look after the surplices, but the question of having a place to store them was referred to the following meeting. By then, Mr Heighway had offered to purchase a cupboard for this purpose at his own expense, and it was also agreed that *"each Member of the Choir (who is able to do so) be required to wash their own surplice"*. It was also agreed that the concert should be postponed until 1 March, *"the time first proposed…having been found insufficient for getting up the music"*.

The Minutes of 1881 start with an interesting record of a choirboy who, having been suspended from the All Saints' Church for three months, wished to join the choir at S. Chad's as a probationer. (The reason for his suspension was that on the evening of the First Sunday after Christmas Day, he went, in company with others, carol-singing instead of attending Church; several pages are taken up with this matter.)

It was agreed in May that the piano should be tuned for the concert (now scheduled for 23 June), and that the surplices (including those *"in the box"*) be washed for Whit Sunday. Mr Penn also suggested that each of the boys should be furnished with a short prayer (to be inserted into their Chant Books) to be used on entering and leaving Church.

It is recorded in June that a letter had been received from the Churchwardens, and the committee's response was that *"Mr Penn chose the tunes from Hymns Ancient & Modern and would be glad to hear from the Churchwardens of any tunes he had omitted which the congregation were familiar with, and, if they desired it, Mr Penn would be pleased to confer with them personally upon the subject".*

On 24 June 1881 Walter Hay wrote a letter to the Churchwarden, Mr Onions, asking for clarification about how he was to receive his salary in future (1048/4897):

My dear Mr Onions,
As I am not sure how you will conduct the finances of the Parish, I write to ask you. Mr Wotton used to send my cheques on the quarter day and I used to send a receipt to Mr Richard and he sent a cheque.
I will do as you like, I have given Mr Green my receipt for £10 and £4.8.6. If you do not send the cheques by this perhaps you will send word when I am to send.
Yours very faithfully,
Walter C Hay

It is hoped that the matters were sorted satisfactorily!

At the AGM in July, a letter from the Vicar recorded his regret in not being able to be present, but at the same time expressed his *"hearty thanks for the Choir's perseverance and successful efforts"*; and his desire to become a contributor to the Choir Excursion which, he hoped, would take place shortly. It was resolved *"that we the members of the Choir assembled do desire to tender our hearty thanks to Mr Penn our Choirmaster for the care and pains he has bestowed upon us during the past twelve months, and we desire to express our full appreciation of his self-denying efforts and kindly treatment of us all, as also our conviction that the progress we have made is mainly due to him"*. It was hoped that the concert (which had been *"in preparation for some time"*) would have taken place in June, but the many *"hindrances to practice"* (i.e. bad attendance) which had occurred had made the committee decide to postpone it until the winter months.

The Churchwardens must have felt that something should be done about the old Gray organ (which was presumably the Wingfield organ from twenty years earlier), as, in September 1881, Mr Onions received a letter from Gray & Davison Ltd, Organ Manufactory, 18 Colquitt Street, Liverpool (1048/1363):

Dear Sirs,
The dirty state of your Organ is not satisfactory for its proper preservation.
We have pleasure in sending Estimate as requested
To Clean the Instrument thoroughly, taking out all the pipes, doing nessasary [sic] repair, & regulate the whole will cost £26 – 18 – 0
This is the lowest cost for the proper preservation.

The organ builders also mentioned the advantage of having a *"new Swell"* which could *"be placed anywhere"*, at the cost of £124, a low price (*"cut fine"*) to induce the church to have it done at the same time as the Bellow (sic).

On 8 September, Walter Hay wrote to Mr Onions (1048/1364) with the following request:

> *If you decide upon having the organ cleaned, I should be glad if you could at the same time have a <u>coupler</u> put in to <u>couple</u> the choir to the <u>Swell</u> organ.*
>
> *I am Dear Sir,*
> *Yours very faithfully.*
> *Walter C Hay*

Frustratingly, there is no record about the decisions made or the action taken.

The Annual Treat held that month was an excursion to Grinshill, and at a meeting held a few weeks later Mr Penn proposed that there should be an examination of Trebles and Altos *"with a view to the re-arrangement of the parts of the Choir"*.

In October, the Vicar and Wardens resolved that *"copies of Hymns Ancient & Modern should be gratuitously supplied to the Choir and Congregation, the same to be considered as an Appendix to the present Hymn Book. A general desire was expressed that a better selection of Hymns should be made in the future, and that such Hymns and Tunes should be selected as might be more within the compass of the congregation generally"*.

The following month, three boys were requested to attend a meeting to be told that their voices were *"undergoing a change and it was thought advisable to ask them (for their own good) to retire from the Choir until their voices were entirely settled either to Tenor or Bass, and then, if their voices were approved of, to rejoin the choir again"*. They were given small presents in recognition of their past services.

By March 1882, a date had been chosen for the much-awaited choir concert; it would take place on 25 May with a repeat performance on the following day. A proposal from Mr Penn that a Mr John Wotton, Jnr, be asked to contribute a little instrumental music was carried.

There seem to have been ongoing complaints about the selection of Hymns, as, following a short discussion on the subject on 19 June, the committee resolved that *"the question be left in the hands of Mr Penn, and report at a future meeting the result of his exertions in the matter"*.

Rather surprisingly, the Choir was presented with a set of handbells in September; Mr Penn and two gentlemen were appointed to confer with the donor as to the Rules whereby they were to be dedicated to their use. Later that month, a further three boys were regretfully asked *"to resign their places in the Choir, owing to their voices being so unsettled"*. Fortunately there was a supplementary class of boys who attended the practices regularly, from which replacements were *"forth-coming to supply any falling off"* which occurred from time to time.

On 8 January 1883, the Committee agreed (subject to the approval of Mr Penn) that the Choir should attend the Festival at S. Mary's Church later in the year, but this decision was rescinded the following week. Mr Penn took over as Chairman at this time and remained in post until July 1884.

The AGM Report of July 1883 not only mentions the proposed new choir stalls (gifted by Mr Heighway, Churchwarden), but also the reopening of the church, which seemed to the committee to be a convenient time to adopt the rendition of 'full Choral Service in the Parish'. The choir moved down into the church from the gallery, and the old stalls were offered for sale. Oak (rather than pitch-pine which would have been £5 cheaper) was chosen for the new choir stalls; Churchwarden Mr Heighway *"announced his desire to present choir stalls to the church in memory of his business partner, the late Mr. John Humphreys"*.

The Committee recommended that an acknowledgement of their appreciation should be sent to Mr Heighway to thank him for his *"great liberality"* and for the *"deep interest that he had ever manifested towards the Choir"*.

Only two meetings (both in May 1884) seem to have occurred in the year to the next AGM. At the first, it was resolved that *"one of the Adult Members should in future collect the Alms from the Choir in a bag provided for that purpose"*, and at the second the suggestion of *"establishing a bye-law prohibiting strangers or friends from taking part in the choir on Sundays"* was referred to a future Meeting. Mention is also made of some services being held at **old** S. Chad's Church at this time.

Of interest is the copy of a letter sent by the Choir's Registrar to Mr Heighway (as Senior Warden) on 16 May:

It having come to the knowledge of the members of the Choir that a change of Organist is imminent at St Chad's Church, I am commissioned to convey the following request to you as Senior Warden of the Parish, in order that you may lay the same before the Clergy and your Colleagues for favourable consideration.

The self sacrificing and earnest manner in which Mr Penn has performed for so long a time the functions of instructor to the Choir entitles him to due recognition as an Official of the Church, and as we are informed that the duties of the present Organist, as at present arranged, include the function of Choirmaster we respectfully urge that in making any fresh appointment the functions of Choirmaster and Organist shall be made distinct from each other, and that the former shall be conferred upon Mr Penn in a duly registered Minute of the Vestry. Of course we mean that his position shall continue honorary as heretofore.

I forbear to comment upon the justice of our request as I feel sure that the gratitude felt to Mr Penn for his kind services is not confined to Members of the Choir, and I feel convinced that those I am now addressing will feel as much pleasure as any of us if it is in their power to make his position firmer and more permanent amongst us.

The next Organist of S. Chad's was Benjamin Pritchard and historians are very fortunate that his contract of employment (*"An Agreement as the duties of Organist between the Vicar and Wardens and Mr Benjamin Pritchard"*) is preserved in the Shropshire Archives (1048/4898):

(Seal) An Agreement made this second day of November one thousand eight hundred and eighty four Between The Reverend John Yardley Vicar of the Parish Church of St Chad Shrewsbury and Samuel Heighway, Herbert Major, Henry Meeson Morris and Robert Waltkins Churchwardens of the said parish (hereinafter called the said Vicar and Churchwardens of the one part) and Benjamin Pritchard of Shrewsbury aforesaid Professor of Music of the other part.

Whereas the said Vicar and Churchwardens have duly elected the said Benjamin Pritchard Organist of the said Parish Church of Saint Chad at and under the salary hereinafter mentioned and, subject to the following stipulations Now it is hereby agreed between the said Vicar, Churchwardens and the said Benjamin Pritchard as follows that is to say

1. The said Benjamin Pritchard shall well and faithfully discharge the duties of Organist of the said Parish Church to the satisfaction of the Vicar and Churchwardens for the time being of the said parish.

2. The duties of the said office shall commence on the second day of November 1884.

3. The said Benjamin Pritchard shall personally attend all services and rehearsals and perform the duties of Organist at such times as shall be required by the Vicar for the time being of the said parish and shall not absent himself without the previous consent of the Vicar for the time being.

4. The said Benjamin Pritchard shall have the privilege of using the Organ in the said parish church for instruction of his pupils on obtaining the written consent of the Vicar and Senior Warden.

5. The salary of the said Benjamin Pritchard shall be the sum of Forty Pounds and shall be paid by the said Churchwardens for the time being on the 25th day of March, the 24th day of June, the 29th day of September and the 25th day of December, the first payment to be made on the 25th day of March next.

6. The said Benjamin Pritchard shall also be entitled to receive in addition to the said salary all the endowments or emoluments attached to the office of Organist of the said parish church at such times as are provided by the trusts or other sources out of which such endowments and emoluments are payable.

7. This Agreement may be determined by the Vicar and Churchwardens for the time being or the said Benjamin Pritchard giving at any time to the other or others of them three calendar months notice in writing to determined the same.

In witness Whereof the said parties to these presents have hereunto set their hands the day and year first above written.

Signed by the said

John Yardley

Samuel Heighway

Herbert Major

In the presence of Henry Meeson Morris

+ witness Robert Waltkins

+ witness Benjamin Pritchard

At the first meeting after Mr Pritchard's appointment (though, as Organist only, he was not present at it), Mr Penn spoke of the irregularity of attendance of some members of the choir, and it was resolved that he should *"interview and warn … any members he thought proper, and if necessary instruct the Secretary to write and inform them that their further services would not be required."* There followed a discussion about the scarcity of books (which had been much complained about amongst the choir!) and it was agreed that *"each member should have a set of his own and, in the case of special music being performed, each member should be provided with a copy for his use during practice and Service".*

The wardens were requested to grant permission for the erection of a second Surplice Cupboard on the opposite side of the Vestry to the one already existing. Most relevantly, Mr Penn undertook to see the *"newly-appointed Organist Mr Pritchard, with a view to secure the services of the accompanist for the practices who plays at the Sunday Services".*

Members of the Choir continued to receive serviceable editions of Hymns Ancient & Modern on their resignation over the next few years.

There is an intriguing comment in the Minutes of 13 July 1885 when the Committee offered *"a sincere vote of condolence to Mr C Penn"*; despite searching the official GRO for that quarter, no death records of any close members of his family have been identified.

The next Minutes date from a short meeting in August 1886 at which the plans for the Annual Treat on 5 September were discussed. In December, it was resolved that the *"cost of the Boys Cassocks be defrayed out of the Choir Fund".*

Discipline was as strict as ever in 1887 when, as a punishment for incessant talking during Service, six boys had 20 merit marks deducted, and certain boys lost anything from 5 to 30 marks for misconduct; it was noted, however, that extra marks in proportion (though not to exceed 20) could be gained by attending extra services. A few months later, Mr Penn kindly proposed that *"all Boys who have bad marks against their names for the present Quarter, the same to be remitted in commemoration of H.M.*

the Queen's Jubilee". He also proposed a concert to defray the costs of that year's summer outing to Ellesmere, but there is no record of whether that concert ever took place.

It was resolved in April 1888 that a notice should be posted in the Vestry, reminding members that "*unless the Services and Practices are attended more regularly, the Choirmaster will adopt stringent measures*". The annual outing was to Bridgnorth, starting at 8.00am after Matins at 7.30am, and the "*necessary brakes for conveying the choir*" were engaged from a Mr Franklin.

The Reverend E S Carpenter was instituted on 5 August 1888; the living had been vacated on the death of the Reverend John Yardley after an incumbency of fifty two years. Within four days of the institution, a Vestry meeting stated that it was "*his wish and the wish of the Bishop, Archdeacon and Rural Dean that the pulpit be moved from its present position to the corner of the chancel and a lectern placed in the other corner and the altar be raised and the chancel extended, that the pews be made lower and the doors taken off. A credence table and other furniture necessary for the reverend celebration of Holy Communion should be purchased and a faculty was applied for.*" Hymn boards had also appeared for the first time in S. Chad's by December 1888. Perhaps the Oxford Movement of 1833 had at last made its mark on this church. It seems that in a further faculty of 1893 the choir stalls were again remodelled.

It is interesting to see that, for the first time it seems since his appointment (nearly four years previously), the name of Benjamin Pritchard is amongst those attending a choir committee meeting; there was no mention of music at all as the whole of the meeting was taken up with discussion about getting subscriptions for a Wedding Present for the Rev. C R Durham who was about to leave the parish!

The organ must have been giving yet more cause for concern as in August 1889, Nicholson & Lord (later Nicholson & Son), Organ Builders, Vicarage Place, Walsall, sent the following quote for repair/addition:

£15-10/- 1. taking Bellows out do repairs absolutely necessary
£24 2. + releathering them entirely
£34 3. + putting the Choir Chest right which has been damaged by the rain
£158 4. + provides for a new Swell Organ:
Bourdon double Diapason
Open Diapason
Stopped Diapason
Viol d'Amore
Vox Celeste
Principal
15
Mixture
Cornopean
Hautboy
Cannot enlarge present Swell
Tubular Pneumatic system

The Churchwardens went for option 3; their letter, dated 7 September 1889, explaining that they were *"not in a position to do other as they were about to enlarge the chancel, put in clergy stalls and several other alterations at considerable expense. Please do by 3 October (Harvest) or start after"*.

Unsurprisingly, the work was <u>not</u> done by the beginning of October, and the churchwardens received the invoice dated 9 December which had the following hopeful request from the Organ Builder: *"If you could do this without inconvenience between now and Saturday, it would be very useful for me"*!

At the end of 1889, the committee decided to collect money from choir members to be expended upon a pair of Candlesticks as their Gift to the Church. It was agreed that *"the boy members of the Choir should for the future be limited to ten either side, and the probationers to four"*.

The lighting for the Choir Stalls was giving concern, so it was resolved in 1890 that the Vicar should write to the Churchwardens about it. A temporary gas bracket was fitted but this still proved unsatisfactory. At the end of that year there is mention that the conduct of several adult members and boys during service and while entering church necessitated the Vicar's speaking to them on the subject.

The first meeting of 1891 resolved to look into the state of the books and surplices. It was also agreed that whenever boys were *"raised from their stalls into the men's that they be not allowed to attend Committee Meetings of the Choir until they are proposed and the resolution carried."*

The outing of 1892 was discussed at length in May of that year; the boys were to be given the choice as to whether they would rather accompany the men to Oxford or go on a different day to Liverpool. Later that month, the Librarian was instructed to purchase a 'Cyclostyle' (a writing implement with a small toothed wheel to cut small holes in a stencil) for his use.

The New Guide to Shrewsbury, published in 1893, describes the organ in S. Chad's as *"a fine instrument by Messrs Gray and Davidson of London"*, though presumably now in the care of Nicholson and Lord who had carried out work as above. 1893 also saw the faculty being approved not only *"for lowering the choir stall"* but also for making an *"outside way to the stoke-hole"* which had formerly been approached though an arch in the choir vestry. In June of that year, after discussing four possible places of interest, the choir decided to visit Bridgnorth for their annual outing.

In July 1894, they travelled to Aberystwyth, having decided against Barmouth at a meeting in June; the long train journey necessitated a very early start of 3.40am, and it was agreed that *"Breakfast be included in the day's Menu"*!

It is interesting to note that the Minutes of that June meeting have been signed later as a correct record by Benjamin Pritchard, described as Choirmaster and Chairman. The date of Mr Penn's cessation as Choirmaster is unrecorded, but the last mention of his name in the list of those present at committee meetings is 26 November 1888, when he was still a few years short of his 50th birthday. He and his wife and family are recorded on the censuses of 1891 and 1901, but he died in his mid-sixties, on 9 May 1907, leaving effects of £1,398 9s 7d. One will never know if there was friction between him and the new Organist of the church.

The first meeting of 1895 records a resolution that *"the Choir undertake the getting up of 'The Crucifixion' for Good Friday, and that Monday Evenings form a Special Practice for the same"*. It was also noted that the Bishop had expressed a desire to entertain the members of the Choir to Supper, Tuesday 15 January being decided on as a convenient day. The adoption of the amended Choir Rules was carried on 10 May, and the destination for the annual choir outing in July was agreed to be Llandudno. The choir again went to Aberystwyth for their outing in 1896, and in 1897 journeyed to Blackpool.

Tenders for the redecoration of the church were invited in June 1903, and while the work was being done, all the services were held in the Music Hall, which was hired outright for a month. The following invoices are in relation to the music and to other matters of interest:

- from Adnitt & Naunton (Booksellers and Bookbinders), The Square:
  "June 23 1903 100   Hymn Books @ 1/3 = £4/5/0"
  (Shropshire Archives 1048/1690)

- from Shrewsbury Music Hall Co Ltd, The Square:
  "for Hire of Music Hall,

Aug 9	£2-2-0
Aug 16	£2-2-0
Aug 23	£2-2-0
	£6-6-0

  (rec. William H Smith)"   (1048/1694)

- *"29 Aug 1903 extra church cleaning – 5 women @2/6 per day = £3-15-0"* (1048/1704)

- from F W Ebrall – Organ Builder, Abbey Foregate:
  "19 Sept 1903, To use of Music Hall Organ 3 Sundays £2
  Water for Blowing 8/-"   *(1048/1708)*

F W Ebrall was a very well-known local Organ Builder, and his younger brother was to become Organist of S. Chad's within a few years.

It is also interesting to note that there is also an invoice (1048/1697) dated January 1904 for supplies from Pritchard & Sons, Nurserymen, Florists and Seedsmen, 9 Shoplatch – i.e. the organist Benjamin Pritchard's father and brothers.

As stated at the outset, information about the organs and music of S. Chad's is scarce and confused. One report states that Commander (Colonel?) Wingfield's organ of 1861 had been declared unfit for further repair some years previously, but reference is still being made to the old Gray organ of 1848 (which must be one and the same instrument).

There was also an invoice from F W Ebrall (Organ Builder, & Co.) (Shropshire Archives 1048/1709) which states:

"*Mar 10 1904: "St. Chad's Church Organ – To Tuning same from Easter 1903-1904 £4- Received with thanks for F W Ebrall, S B Ebrall 29 Mar '04"*

However, everything was to change within a few months. The church, probably persuaded by its Organist, Benjamin Pritchard, who was doubtless fed up with the constant problems which the organ had given, decided to purchase a brand new instrument from the Norwich firm of Norman & Beard; this completely broke with Shrewsbury tradition. At that time, this company was one of the largest and most up-to-date organ builders in the world. Their craftsmanship was excellent and much of what they installed in S. Chad's then is still in use today.

It is uncertain what happened to the old organ, but what is certain is that no part of it was used in the new instrument. It has been suggested that it was removed to S. George's Church, Pontesbury, but other reports suggest that the former instrument from the Music Hall was installed there. It is possible that neither instrument found its way to Pontesbury!

Interestingly, there is, amongst the many invoices for 1904, one dated 3 June for *"removing snow"*(!), as well as others for *"making and washing surpluses* [sic] *@ 9d each"* and *"getting in the coke"*. The churchwardens also gave £10 to the bellringers, and £3-15s-0d to the steeple keepers. But the major item of expenditure was £400 due on 1 October: the deposit for the new organ.

A letter of 11 August from Norman and Beard to The Venerable Charles Maude (Vicar and Archdeacon of Salop) states that the organ builders were *"gratified on the decision"* that their estimate had been accepted. They also wrote: *"You may rest assured that we shall spare no effort to make the Instrument, in all respects, a complete success"* (Shropshire Archives 1048/1412).

In consultation with the builders, Benjamin Pritchard arranged certain alterations to the specification. It was also agreed that the old organ was not to be removed until the new one was ready for delivery, at which time a further £500 was payable, with the balance (less an allowance of £250 for the old organ) due *"on completion to Mr Pritchard's satisfaction"*. The entry to the organ was to be from the back, not from the side (resulting in losing only about four sittings each side); there would be two archways (one to the entrance, and one to the music space); the gallery floor would be levelled, and the old casework would be used for the sides with the rest toned to match.

Norman & Beard wrote: *"We the undersigned undertake to build and erect an organ in St. Chad's Church using only the best materials and workmanship as set forth in the specification"* [q.v.] for a total of £1530.

An invoice dated 31 December from the Gas Light Office, Pride Hill (Shropshire Archives 1048/1786) includes *"Taking down Organ Brackets"* (1/6) on 28 October. It may be of incidental interest that the gas bill from The Shrewsbury Gaslight Company for the three months from October to December was £8-2-10.

In the run up to Christmas, the *"new straps to the Harmonium in Church"* had been repaired (at a cost of 1/6) by E F Allen & Sons Ltd, 68 Mardol. This firm advertised themselves as *"Sole Agents for the*

World Famed Pianos by C Bechstein, Maker to HM The King – Pianos, organs and all kinds of Musical Instruments on Sale or Hire, Tuned and Repaired on Moderate Terms, or Received in Exchange". 39 copies of 'Come let us sing' (and the same number of an unspecified 'Magnificat & Nunc Dimittis') were purchased from them, and possibly collected by hand as *"No music exchanged after it has been passed through the post".*

Various invoices from 1905 relate to the installation of the new organ. These include:

- Thomas Morris, Builder & Contractor, S. Austin Friars, for the *"construction of the new floor £53-9-10"* (Shrewsbury Archives 1048/1377). The girders for the floor weighed 1 ton 14 cwt 2 q.
- Lea, Son & Co, Electricians, for the electric light to the organ, plus *"a carpenter in the motor room (@ 10d per hour)"* (Shropshire Archives 1048/1381), and supplies of *"1 pt of oil for motor and 1 tin of commudine"* (Shropshire Archives 1048/1386)
- Norman & Beard, for *"extra for screen at the back of the organist"* (Shropshire Archives 1048/1387)
- HE Lloyd Oswell, Dana Chambers, for *"strengthening the gallery: £7-7s-0d!"* (Shropshire Archives 1048/1389)

There were also the legal fees in the Consistory Court of Lichfield for the *"Professional Charges of and incidental to the preparation of the petition for Faculty"* totalling £3-3-0 (Shropshire Archives 1048/1798)

The Faculty (Shropshire Archives 1048/1555) is dated 13 February 1905:

(Seal)

<u>*To all Christian People*</u> *to whom these Presents shall come, We GEORGE JOHN TALBOT, Esquire, Master of Arts, VICAR GENERAL of the Honourable and Right Reverend Father in God Augustus, by Divine Permission Lord Bishop of Lichfield, and OFFICIAL PRINCIPAL of the EPISCOPAL CONSISTORY COURTOF LICHFIELD, lawfully constituted;*

SEND GREETINGS:

Whereas it has been represented unto Us by and on the part and behalf of The Venerable Charles Bulmer Maude Vicar of Saint Chad's Shrewsbury and Archdeacon of Salop within the Diocese of Lichfield and William Major John Davis Samuel Heighway and William Smith the Churchwardens of the said Parish of Saint Chad's Shrewsbury That it is desired to erect a New Organ in the same position as the Old one in the Parish Church of Saint Chad's Shrewsbury aforesaid in accordance with the designs of Messieurs Norman and Beard of Norwich. That the Cost of the said work is estimated at one thousand four hundred and fifty pounds and that the same is to be defrayed by the sale of the Old Organ to Messieurs Norman and Beard for two hundred pounds and by subscription. That the said work will involve in addition to the removal of the Old Organ the removal of about twelve sittings. That the said work has been unanimously approved by the Parishioners in Vestry and that there is no Lay Rector for the said Parish.

AND, WHEREAS the said Petitioners have prayed our Licence, or Faculty, for the purposes aforesaid – KNOW YE NOW THEREFORE that we desiring to comply with the reasonable request of the said Petitioners (the due Forms and Orders of Law in this case requisite having been first had and observed), DO GRANT this our LICENCE, or FACULTY, to the effect and in manner hereinbefore mentioned, PROVIDED ALWAYS that if it shall be necessary in carrying out the said work to remove or disturb any Vaults, Graves, Tombstones, or Monuments, due care shall be had thereof, and any Bodies or Remains there may be found shall be decently re-interred within Consecrated Ground, under the Superintendence of the Incumbent and Churchwardens for the time being, and the Monuments, or Tombstones replaced in a suitable position. IN TESTIMONY whereof We have caused the Seal of our office to be hereunto affixed this Thirteenth day of February in the Year of Our Lord One Thousand Nine Hundred and Five

Hubert C Hodson
Registrar

It is just as well that this faculty was granted, as two days later, the Vicar, Archdeacon Maude, dedicated the new organ on 15 February 1905. The event began with the singing of 'The Old Hundredth' unaccompanied and then two further hymns were sung: 'O praise ye the Lord' and 'Praise the Lord, ye heavens adore him'. A solo, 'O come, let us worship' was performed by Mr T O Boulton, and the church choir (augmented by singers from other church choirs in the town) sang Dykes' 'Festival Te Deum'. At the conclusion of the service, Mr C W Perkins, the noted Organist of Birmingham Town Hall, played Wagner's 'Overture to Tannhäuser'. Mr Perkins also gave the inaugural recital to an *"overflowing congregation"* which included the Mayor and Corporation. The programme was as follows:

Allegro in D	Handel
Fantasia and Fugue in C minor	J S Bach
Meditation	Kleine
Toccato (sic) on 'An Ancient Hebrew Melody'	Faulkes
Scherzo in 5/4 time	Bernard
Finale on 'A Stronghold Sure'	Mendelssohn

Mr Perkins gave a further recital after the following Sunday's evening service. According to the *Shrewsbury Chronicle* the organ contained *"all that was new in organ building"* (hardly surprising, in that Norman & Beard were one of the most innovative organ builders of that time). It cost £1500 of which £500 still needed to be paid, and the collection at the service realised £30 towards this. It is interesting to note that the *Chronicle* commented on the beautiful quality of the Vox Humana and Orchestral Oboe stops, both of which subsequently disappeared in later work on the organ! Other associated invoices included:

- A Pritchard, Printer, 2 Mardol, for 1,500 programmes (2 sides - organ recital): £1-3-6

- Langworth Wilding, Printer, 35 Castle Street, for Organ Fund stationery including 100 postcards, 1,000 "I will subscribe" slips, as well as advertisements in the 'Wellington Journal' and 'Shrewsbury Chronicle', and notices, tickets and flags: £7-10-5

A receipt from this time (Shropshire Archives 1048/1790), signed by Benjamin Pritchard, shows that the organist's salary was now £15 per quarter.

Normal church life continued after the opening of the new organ. Music was bought (including Cathedral Psalters and Chant Books, plus 32 copies of 'Holy Offerings'), and Mrs E Grindlay continued her sterling work of *"washing 39 Quire Surpluses @ 6d each plus 2 Clergy Surpluses @ 9d each"* in the six days prior to Christmas Day 1905.
(Shropshire Archives 1048/1819)

The Choir continued to thrive, and seemed to enjoy a good musical and social life. Outings were held in the summers of 1907 (Southport) and 1908 (Llandudno) and below is an example of a letter inviting participants. [this one addressed to a 'Mr W A Smith', possibly the churchwarden William Smith] (Shropshire Archives 1048/4947):

---

10 Claremont Hill
25 June 1907

Dear Sir,
I am desired by the Committee of the Choir to invite your Company to the Annual Choir 'Outing' on July 8th to Southport.

I should be glad if you will kindly let me know as early as convenient.

Yours very truly,
A Lane
(Hon Sec)

In the Archives are various invitations to services held at the church in 1910, such as the 'Lantern Service' on Good Friday at 8.00pm. Guests were also *earnestly invited to attend* the 'Service of Thanksgiving for Peace' on Sunday 6 July at 6:30pm, which involved 45 bandsmen, 40 officers and 4 other KSLI soldiers from Copthorne Barracks.

It is difficult to pinpoint exactly when Pritchard relinquished his duties as Organist of S. Chad's, and consequently it is unclear when the next Organist, Walter Browning Ebrall began his employment, but we do know that he was in post by early 1911, and it is likely that he was appointed at least a year before that date.

Ebrall was obviously an excellent organist (gaining his ARCO) and choirmaster; local newspaper articles from his earlier years at S. Chad's write highly of his direction of pieces such as Stainer's 'Crucifixion' (which was, from 1911, performed <u>twice</u> each Lent by S. Chad's Choir under his direction) as well as various organ recitals, e.g.

- Shrewsbury Chronicle - 5 April 1912 [Good Friday]: *"The choir of St. Chad's Church Shrewsbury repeated their rendering of Stainer's Crucifixion on Sunday afternoon before a large congregation. As on the previous Thursday, the music was beautifully sung – both the choir and choirmaster (Mr W B Ebrall, ARCO) deserving high praise for their efforts."*

- Shrewsbury Chronicle – 3 January 1913: *"On Sunday evening, at St. Chad's Church Shrewsbury, the organist (Mr W B Ebrall, ARCO) gave an enjoyable recital assisted by Mr E C Marshall. Special music was sung at Matins, including the anthem 'With all thy hosts' (West) which had a most effective rendering."*

In the latter edition, there was also an advertisement by Shrewsbury Choral Society who wanted to recruit new singers in the hope of having more than 200 members.

Christmas Day was a very busy day in the calendar for church workers, the services advertised in 1910 being as follows:

Holy Communion: 6 a.m.; 7 a.m.; 8 a.m. CHORAL
Mattins & Holy Communion: 11 a.m.
Children's Service: 2:45 p.m.
Evensong & Carols: 6:30 p.m.

(Shropshire Archives 1048/4948)

It seems that a lot of amateur music events took place in the parish in the days before the Great War; but how many were arranged by Walter or involved the church choir is impossible to tell. Entertainment (including popular songs, band-music, recitations and drama) would take place at Parish Teas, and at events held in the Music Hall in aid of church organisations such as the S. Chad's Boys' and Young Men's Clubs and Camp. Well-known artistes (such as 'Mr Emlyn Davies, the eminent Welsh Baritone') would offer their services to the cause, and the events would be advertised with structured ticket pricing (for example, 3/6 for reserved and numbered seats and 10/6 for a family ticket to admit 4, 3/0 for the first row of the balcony with all other seats being 2/0).

A letter from C R Wingfield detailing the protocol (Shropshire Archives 1048/4954-6) for a civic service on 13 January 1912 (at which Lord Powis and Lord Clive were to be present) mentions 45 officers and 35 ladies and gives strict instructions that *"on no account let anyone in mufti sit among them"*!

The Reverend F W Greenwood, DD was instituted as Vicar on 22 July 1913 and the bells were rededicated on Wednesday 27 May 1914; the Order of Service for the latter shows that this was in the form of Evensong, with the music including Psalms 84 and 150, Hymns 292, 550 and 'Lifted high within the steeple' (on a sheet), but no choir anthem was listed, nor was there any mention of the organ voluntaries.

Similarly there are no real details of the music included in the Royal Salop Infirmary's Anniversary Services which took place in January each year usually in the presence of high-powered clergy; the three hymns in 1919 and 1920 were nos. 201 ('Gracious Spirit, Holy Ghost'), 365 ('Thou, to Whom the sick and dying') and 369 ('Thine arm, O Lord'), and, although the Te Deum was also sung, no composers' names are listed.

Walter Ebrall resigned in 1933 and was succeeded by Austin Herbert. During Austin's time the records of the musical life of S. Chad's are more numerous than in the previous twenty- five years, and it is possible to glean some idea of what church life was like in the years leading up to World War II.

24 September 1933: Jane Clayton, 13 Claremont P, Claremont Hill –

"For repairing 31 Assocks [sic]:	*15 / 0*
Bills	*7 / 9*
Thread	*<u>10</u>*
	1 / 3 / 7"

18 July 1934: Wm Hill & Son, and Norman & Beard Ltd, 372 York Road, London N7 - £12 for *"tuning and regulating the organ for one year ended 24/6/34"* (Shropshire Archives 1048/3560-1)

Wilfred Thomasson, Melias Chambers, 65 Mardol – £16-10 *"To oiling [organ] motor for half year to end July 1934"* (1048/3528)

Petty cash disbursements include 1/- for *"1 Book – organ pupils"* and 3/6 for *"2 boxes (large) drawing pins for marking reserved seats"*! (Shropshire Archives 1048/3578)

There is a lengthy invoice (Shropshire Archives 1048/3616) from Thomas Morris & Sons, Builders and Contractors dated August 1934 regarding the 'Organ in gallery':

"Additional roof ceiling in roof pace above organ

Materials:

480ft 4x2 deal	*4 – 0 – 0*
570ft 1" deal board	*7 – 6 – 6*
145ft eaves spar	*1 – 4 – 6*
20lb nuts	*4 – 2*
6lb clout nails, 1 hasp & staple	*2 - 6*
6 Rolls of roofing felt	*1 –10 – 0*
2 tins of solution, 4lb of solder	*9 – 0*

Labour:

	hrs:	
16th: Foreman	*12*	*1 – 4 – 0*
carpenter	*42*	*3 –13 –6*
"	*40*	*3 – 0 – 0*
labourer	*20*	*1 – 5 – 0*

plumber	10	17 – 6
23rd: Foreman	8	16 – 0
carpenter	43	3 –15 – 3
"	43	3 – 4 – 6
labourer	20	1 – 5 – 0
		£33 – 13 – 5 "

17 August 1934: Reginald R Fisk, Hartley Street Works, Wolverhampton - £20/-/- *"To first instalment on account or work etc. to the Organ".* (The second and third instalments were invoiced one and two weeks later.) (Shropshire Archives 1048/3574)

25 September: Wilfred Thomasson, Electrical engineer and contractor, radio specialist: *"attending organ, oiling motor and all bearings, etc. (no charge – contract), refixing lamp standards in choir stalls, also to supplying and fixing lamps:*
> *2 210/60w pearl @ 1/9*
> *2 150w clear BC @ 5/-*
> *2 150w clear EC @ 5/- "* (Shropshire Archives 1048/3585)

27 September: Livesey Limited, Printer, St. John's Hill:
> *"750 pence envelopes 2½ x 4¼ printed in black 'Organ Fund' – 7/9"*
> (Shropshire Archives 1048/3624)

S. Chad's Autumn Cleaning: *"5 women @ 4/- a day for six days, 1 man @ 6/- for four days"* (Shropshire Archives 1048/3584)

September: L E Darling – *"Bill for Ruffs (laundered) for Boys:*   *10/-*
                           20 collars: *5/-"* (1048/3587)

The Boys' Merit List for the Quarter ending 29 Sept 1934 was for £2-14-11. (Shropshire Archives 1048/3602)

30 September: Sabrina Laundry, Longden Coleham for *"Laundry of Surplices July and Sept -*
July:	*20 Boys*	*10/-*
Sept:	*19 Boys*	*9/6*
	12 Men	*9/-*
		1/8/6 " '

16 October: Wilfred Thomasson – *"To repairing light on organ and supplying new switch, time, etc: 3/6"*

4 November: Boys' Merit Money was 6/6

23 November: to Rev E Moore-Darling (Vicar) and F Austin Herbert Esq, High Croft, Longden Road:

"To repairing 15 Hymn Books and to putting cloth backs on same: £1 – 7 – 6" (1048/3654)

29 November: Reginald Fisk invoiced for £15 on account (Shropshire Archives 1048/3633)

November: Livesey Limited, Printers: *"1,000 LP 8vo single copies 'Form of Service' printed in mauve on white – 15/6"* (Shropshire Archives 1048/3652) These 'forms of service' were forms on which hymns and psalms and anthems and settings were detailed and these continued in use up until the 1970s.

7 December: Sabrina Laundry for *"washing surpluses –*
  22 Boys   11/-
  13 Mens   9/9
  22 Ruffs   4/7
       £1/5/4 " (1048/3642)

22 December: Choir Boys' Pay for the Quarter was £2 – 10 – 4

22 December: to Rev. E Moore Darling from Forrest & Son, Piano and radiogram merchants, 41 Castle Street :

"Nov:		
8 Cathedral Psalters @ 4/-	*1/12/0*	
8 A&M Hymn Books @ 2/6	*1/ 0 /0*	
	2/12/0	
Dec: *36 Short Communion @ 1/-*	*1/16/0*	
36 Te Deum @ 4d	*12/0*	
36 God is Gone up @ 6d	*18/0*	
	3/6/0 " (Shropshire Archives 1048/3653)	

Unfortunately it is not documented as to whose 'Short Communion Service' or 'Te Deum' was purchased, or indeed who was the composer of the anthem 'God is gone up', but it is likely that this was the anthem by Croft, as the church have a set of copies of that piece which probably date from this time.

The next batch of records in the Archives all date from 1940:

An invoice (Shropshire Archives 1048/1459) dated 19 September from Reginald R Fisk (who was now based at 49½ Worcester Street, Wolverhampton and specialising in rebuilding, overhauling, cleaning, tuning and maintenance of electric blowers) re *"Repairs to organ damaged by water entering the roof - £12"* was sent to Messrs MacDonald, S. Chad's Church, Shrewsbury.

It appears that Messrs MacDonald & Co were Church Restoration Specialists, based in Kenrick Road, Mapperley, Nottingham, and they replied to Mr Fisk thus: *"We would say we are not responsible for that invoice, and upon referring to our files, find that we have not authorised you to effect any repairs. Therefore we return your account herewith."* (Shropshire Archives 1048/1460)

Mr Fisk then wrote to T E Gwilliam Esq of 81 Woodfield Road, Shrewsbury asking him to take up the matter with MacDonalds. (Shropshire Archives 1048/1461). However, The Vicar (along with C B Roach) responded on 28 October (Shropshire Archives 1048/1462) saying that there was *"possibly damage by MacDonalds, but little evidence…"*

An invoice for £1,811/5/11 (Shropshire Archives 1048/1463) was received from MacDonalds for the restoration work they had done on the church; however, the solicitors Shayler, Butler & Dilks wrote that they *"held MacDonalds responsible for the damage to the organ"* and that the church should *"deduct it against any money owed"* (Shropshire Archives 1048/1464). This letter is unfortunately the last document relating to church matters held in the Archives, so, regrettably, Messrs. MacDonalds' response to this decision no longer exists.

Austin Herbert resigned his post in 1946 and was succeeded by Reginald Harwood. Music in the next twenty-five years was to be managed with care and extreme diligence.

S. Chad's has been regarded for many years as the 'county church' and this was certainly borne out by several significant Civic Services immediately after the end of the Second World War: a presentation to County Regiments on 31 May 1947 attended by, amongst many others, the Lord Lieutenant of Shropshire, The Right Honourable, The Earl of Powis; the Mayor of Shrewsbury, Dr R H Urwick; the Chairman of the county council, Sir Offley Wakeman; the Mayors of Bridgnorth, Oswestry, Ludlow, Wenlock and Bishops Castle, as well as the Earl of Bradford in his capacity as Hon Colonel of the King's Shropshire Light Infantry and many other high-ranking army officers. On 13 June 1948 the King's Shropshire Light Infantry Memorial Cabinets and books of remembrance were dedicated by The Archdeacon of Salop, The Venerable H S Carpenter. There appears not to have been an anthem at this service, but hymns sung were 'Soldiers of Christ, arise', 'O God, our help in ages past', 'Let saints on earth in concert sing' and 'O valiant hearts' with the National Anthem. At 3.00pm on 6 November 1949 the roll of honour and tablet in memory of men and women of the County of Shropshire who fell in the Second World War (1939-1945) was dedicated by The Right Reverend Robert Hodson, Bishop of Shrewsbury. The anthem at this service was almost certainly 'Holy is the true light' by William Harris.

The church underwent a major redecoration in 1951, and new hymn boards (in memory of Mrs Stewart-White) were added soon afterwards. The Reverend Fred A R Chapman was instituted to the living in 1952 and during his time the choir of men and boys was large and sang each week at Choral Matins and Choral Evensong.

Reg Harwood is remembered warmly by many who knew him as their organ teacher or choir-master. He was a noted teacher of organ. One pupil, Allen Warrender, gives an account: *"He always waited patiently (but anxiously) for any pupil who arrived late for an organ lesson at the church. At that time, [as now], the access to the console was through a little door at the back of the organ, and pupil and teacher had to proceed slowly and carefully through a maze of pipes and sundry music items to get to the front. After dark, it could be extremely eerie, and, in winter, very cold. To ensure that pupils felt their way when playing the pedals, only the manual-light was switched on, and it was only at the end of a lesson that Reg switched on the pedal-light and played a piece."*

Pupils have recalled Reg with affection, as Allen Warrender continues: *"He was a very competent musician, and though humble of his quite obvious talents, played very confidently. He would sit at the console, with his brown brogue shoes and turn-up trousers, oatmeal jacket, playing away in a world of his own. This was his cherished 'baby' and he knew every little sound or quirk it had. He instilled a sense of discipline…that stood me in good stead for other applications in my life. He was a typical church organist – he knew well the strength in his trusty instrument, but was quite happy to be hidden behind the curtain that masked him from the congregation. They too knew well of his talents, but, outside of the immediate clergy, his face was unknown – I feel he was happy with that."*

Throughout his time (and possibly in the days of his two predecessors) organ recitals were given on the days of the famous Shrewsbury Flower Show which is held in the Quarry park adjacent to the church. Each year Reg would play two programmes on each day of the show.

By the late 1950s the organ began to give increasing trouble and it was restored by Nicholson and Company of Worcester in 1963. From 1961 Gilbert Mills was engaged as consultant. Though he worked in insurance, he was a well-known Birmingham organist who was involved in a number of consultations at the time, and frequently broadcast on BBC. Roy Massey described him as " *a wonderful improviser and quite a character"*. Nicholson's submitted an estimate for the work on 31 October 1961 as follows:

Soundboards *The Foot boards and Sliders of the Swell, Great and Choir Soundboards to be removed, and the tables cleaned down and refurbished with Graphite. Footboards to be trued up as required and refurbished. Rackboards to be repaired where required and made secure. Pallets cleaned carefully and springs reset as required after internal pneumatic motors have been releathered and replaced.*

Swell and Choir Boxes *The louvres of the Swell and Choir Boxes to be refitted. Old grease to be removed from the Centres and false movement taken up. The interior of the Boxes to be cleaned, and joints and gaps papered with stout Kraft paper.*

Wind Trunks etc. *All wind trunks to be made sound and free from leaks, and missing screws and flanges replaced.*

Console *The new Console to be of standard Nicholson Drawstop type with panels, jambs and music desk of solid English Oak polished in natural colour. Drawstop Knobs turned from solid Ivory and engraved with Bushes of solid Ivory. Thumb pistons of solid Ivory set in Bushes of Ivory, and Keys covered in Ivory of 8 Cut, laid in one piece without surface joint. Pedal keys of Beech with Rosewood faced sharps set in frame of English Oak. Manual and Pedal Contacts of Gold Alloy set in Bakelite insulating strips, with Coupling Switches of Silver Contacts and enclosed in a Mahogany Cabinet. All Combination Thumb and Toe Pistons to be adjustable at a miniature Switchboard behind the Music Desk. All multi-conductor Cables to be PVC insulated and adequately clipped and protected with Henley Fuse Holders.*

Rectifier *A Kimber-Allen Transformer/Rectifier, with an Output of 30 Amps to be supplied together with a Crabtree contactor switch fitted with overload trip, and controlled by Electric Blower Switch.*

Guarantee *The Organ to be guaranteed against defect due to faulty workmanship or materials for a period of 25 years from the date of completion, provided the care and tuning of the instrument is placed in our hands throughout that time; but no responsibility will be accepted for defects due to Water, Damp, Vermin, Heat or Fire, or any other cause over which we can have no control.*

Note *Free use of Lighting, Heating, Tower, Gas and Water, and Storage for parts of the Organ as may be required to be granted the Organ Builders throughout the progress of the work in the building, and perfect quietness throughout the tonal finishing. All unused materials and parts from the existing Organ to become our property. No Electricians or Builders' work to be undertaken by the Organ Builders in connection with the Electric Blowing Equipment, etc.*

Insurance *Organ parts sent to the factory for overhaul, repair and adaptation to be fully insured by us during the progress of work in our factory; the Church Authorities to be responsible for the insurance of all parts of the Organ undergoing repair in the Church, and for all new organ parts once they are delivered to the Church.*

The faculty which petitioned to the Vicar General of the Diocese, Conolly Hugh Gage from the Vicar, William Johnston and the Churchwardens, Lt Col Gerald Blakeney de Courcy-Ireland, Evan Thomas Powell, John Alfred Forrester and Alfred Harry France read as follows:

- Reconstruction of the Organ in S. Chad's Church, according to the specification of Nicholson and Co (Worcester) Ltd, at a cost of £4,380
- To install a semi-tone bell – i.e a sharp second – in the tower according to the specification of John Taylor and Co (Loughborough) at a cost of £129-1-4
- To make a short, moveable extension to the Altar Rails in the Church (to be placed in the central gap between the existing rails) according to the design of H & K Mabbitt at a cost of £45
- To provide new heating facilities in the vestries of the said church – according to the specification and estimates to be supplied and approved, at an estimated cost of £200.

This faculty was approved by the PCC on 20 March 1962 and submitted to the Diocesan Advisory Committee on 21 May 1962.

The specification of the organ is listed below, and the work was carried out in 1963 as set out above: the tubular pneumatic action was replaced with electro pneumatics and the present very comfortable console of standard Nicholson pattern dates from this time. The opening recital of the restored instrument was given in early 1964 by Melville Cook, Organist of Hereford Cathedral and is remembered as an occasion when the newly restored instrument went wrong during the recital!

From research undertaken by Roy Massey it seems that the rebuilt job was prone to quite a few faults in the early years and then there were serious difficulties when the church put in a new boiler and the temperature in the organ often fluctuated between 46 and 74 degrees according to Reg Harwood. There is a lot of correspondence about the lack of humidity, which resulted in the installation of a humidifier. Perhaps because of rising hot air, the tuning has never been completely stable. It seems that Reg Harwood was a real stickler for the maintenance of the rebuilt organ, as many postcards in the Nicholson files testify. It was also known that he was a generally patient man, but this patience could slip from time to time. The Managing Director of Nicholson's, Mr Lambert, was the master of the soft answer and never seemed to get ruffled, though he could be rather frank about the architects to the church.

Reg Harwood served under five Vicars; Forbes Horan who appointed him, Fred Chapman, William Johnston, Norman Lewis and Christopher Spafford. During Reg's long incumbency the churchmanship of S. Chad's moved 'up the candle', and it seems he felt less comfortable with this increasingly 'catholic' approach. One indication of this is perhaps Reg's wish for Fred Chapman to preach at his retirement evensong at S. Chad's.

Reg was immensely dedicated to his job, remaining in post for twenty five years and generally taking only two Sundays off each year. There were always three (sometimes four) services each Sunday and Reg played for almost all of them, rarely calling in an assistant. He also had a strong discipline with the choir and maintained a healthy top line of boys. There are many who still recall him with affection.

As well as being blessed with fine music, S. Chad's was always at the forefront of liturgical ideas, and it is likely that Reg's innate conservatism often found these things hard to bear. In 1969 'Mission to Shrewsbury' resulted in a visit from the late Jimmy Saville and hymns sung (and accompanied with Reg's usual commensurate skill and professionalism) could not have been to his taste! On 1 November 1970 Ronald Jasper, Chairman of the Church of England's Liturgical Commission (later Dean of York) visited the church to discuss reordering to make the building fit for purpose in the final quarter of the twentieth century. As well as holding a consultation, he preached at the All Saints' Day Eucharist.

Reg was born just a few months after the death of Queen Victoria, and much of his outlook and views were those of a Victorian gentleman. Towards the end of his incumbency, he appeared to become disillusioned with the 'fashionable' ways of the church at that time. He found some of the modern ideas of the curates especially irritating; one in particular (Geoffrey Bostock) was not to his rather modest and retiring taste, and seems to have precipitated Reg's retirement from S. Chad's. Geoffrey was highly skilled at mounting exhibitions and events which enticed many people inside the building for other purposes than for the worship of the Almighty, and Reg found this increasingly difficult. His pupils were never allowed to play the organ above the quietest stops so that anyone who might come into the church for spiritual and religious needs would not be disturbed; he found it less than ideal that people would come in for many reasons which might not be specifically religious.

Reg retired from S. Chad's on Sunday 20 June 1971 and a presentation was made to him and Mrs Harwood in the hall after Evensong.

He wrote in the church newsletter (monthly) for August 1971:

Cairndhu
29 Oakfield Road
Shrewsbury
Sunday 27 June 1971

You very kindly said that you would mention our new address in the August Newsletter. We should be so grateful if you would, at the same time, express our gratitude and appreciation of the kindness and generosity of the S. Chad's folk in giving us such handsome leaving presents.

I hope all is going well today. [NB this letter was written the Sunday after his retirement]

Yours sincerely
Reg Harwood
New address: High Littlefields Close, Wilburton, Ely Cambridgeshire.

As a contingency plan for a possible interregnum after Reg's retirement, David Boarder (Director of Music at the Priory Boys' Grammar School and soon to be Organist of S. Mary's) together with Richard Jones from Shrewsbury School were booked to give several organ recitals over the days of the Flower Show that year.

In the November church newsletter the following appeared:

S. Chad's Vicarage
Shrewsbury

Mr R G Harwood, BMus, FRCO
Many will be shocked and sad to learn of the sudden death of Mr Reginald G Harwood on 19 September 1971. He had been Organist and Choirmaster at S. Chad's for 25 years, and Assistant Director of Music at Shrewsbury School during that period. He only retired last June and he and Mrs Harwood moved their home to Cambridgeshire in July.
Mr Harwood made a great contribution to the worship at S. Chad's, and the musical life of Shrewsbury, where he was Conductor of the Shrewsbury Choral Society and also of the Oswestry Choral Society.
We extend our sympathy to Mrs Harwood and her family.

Yours sincerely
Christopher Spafford.

A Memorial Service for Reg Harwood was held in S. Chad's on Wednesday 6 October, 1971.

Reg's successor was Sam Baker who came to S. Chad's from S. Mary's and who was a very different character. Sam had been a theological student before settling on a musical career, and so had a good understanding of all matters liturgical. He was to revel in all that happened at S. Chad's and increased the church's musical activity significantly. Sam was at S. Chad's for little more than four years, but in this short time he cemented the choral tradition for which S. Chad's has became widely known. He also greatly increased the number of significant concerts held in the venue, setting the musical course which generally continues today. It was under his directorship that the choir toured widely and sang a vastly enhanced repertoire of music from all periods (though excluding music of the later twentieth century which never appealed to Sam's instinctively conservative and romantic tastes). During his time in post, he carved a remarkable musical niche for the church. And yet, in so doing, he managed to harness the support and affirmation of choir, clergy and congregation without any apparent abstention. Everyone seemed keen to support this charismatic figure in his pursuit of excellence (though never elitism). It is perhaps to him more than to anyone else that S. Chad's owes its central role in the musical life of the area.

The commitment of choir members, as well as organists, to the musical life of the church is illustrated in the following example. At around the time of Sam's arrival, a loyal member of the choir, Frank Adams, retired after singing for 75 years. Frank Adams had joined the choir on Christmas Day 1895, aged 8. He was both baptised and later married to his wife, Louise, in the church. Frank lived at 10 Claremont Hill for many years and worked in a land agents' office until 1953. He had taught for four years in S. Chad's Boys' School and had been a member of the church's Sunday School for 68 years. He rarely missed church, and he described a typical Sunday in his early days as Sunday School at 10.00am; church at 11.00am; church at 3.00pm and Evensong at 6.30pm, after which he often helped with the old peoples' service. In his retirement speech Frank praised the *"wonderful clergy and churchwardens and a very happy choir at S. Chad's"* adding *"I have always enjoyed everything I have done"*.

Looking at some of the old choir registers of the 1960s and 1970s, the choir was generally flourishing and hardly went below 18 trebles and a good spread of the ATB parts amongst the men.

Sam Baker initiated a series of concerts 'Music in the Round' (a title which has since been purloined by another organisation, and the current Friday series is now called 'Concerts in the Round'). On Saturday 18 March 1972 the series included an organ recital by Martin How. Martin had been a pupil of Sam's, and was by then well-known through his national work with the Royal School of Church Music. David Leeke spoke to Martin How asking for details of this recital, but unfortunately these are lost. Martin did, however, remember one comment which came from Keith Ross, a family friend of the Bakers and later to be a Lay Clerk at Winchester for many years. He asked Martin why there was no Bach in the programme as he thought it odd to attend an organ recital which didn't contain a piece by the great master. So, although Martin does not recall what he did play on that occasion, he clearly did not play any of the music of J S Bach! A recital by Richard Lloyd, then Organist of Hereford Cathedral, was on

Saturday 6 May, and Martindale Sidwell, of Hampstead Parish Church and S. Clement Danes, played on Saturday 17 June. Other concerts at that time included The Chester S. Cecilia Singers performing music from Gibbons and Hassler to Ireland and Darke. The Reverend Douglas Bean and The Seers performed folk music, and the Liverpool Sandon Orchestra also gave a memorable concert.

It was at this time that a major Festival coinciding with the Shrewsbury Flower Show was established. Exhibitions began in 1969, and vestments worn at Eucharists over these periods were made by Shropshire designers. The 1972 festival saw exhibitions of tapestries by the Benedictine Nuns from Cockfosters; paintings by Christine Slack and Alan Rowlands; vestments from Coventry Cathedral as well as some original designs by Andrew Bond, and ceramics by Mary Fogg. The music programme under Sam's direction was extensive: on Tuesday 15 August a Solemn Eucharist at 6.00pm was sung by the church choir to commemorate the Feast of the Assumption of the Blessed Virgin Mary at which the ordinary of the mass was by Montague Phillips (1885-1969). At 8.00pm that day David Boarder (then Organist of S. Mary's, and also Director of Music at the Priory Boys' Grammar School) gave an organ recital.

On Wednesday 16 August S. Mary's Choir sang Choral Evensong (in S. Chad's) at 6.00pm with works by Batten, Dyson and Hilton. Gerard Doyle, who was a lecturer at S. Martin's College of Education Lancaster, gave a violin recital at 8.00pm with works by Veracini, Sweelinck, Mozart and Dvorak. On Thursday 17 August there was a concert of music for recorders and harpsichord. The Shrewsbury Chamber Singers sang at a Solemn Eucharist at 6.00pm: the mass ordinary was 'The Western Wynde' by John Taverner; the Gradual: 'Let thy merciful ears' by Mudd, the Offertory: 'Purge me, O Lord' by Tallis; the Communion: 'Drop, drop, slow tears' by Gibbons. That day concluded with a piano recital by John James who was Director of the Royal Normal College for the Blind. He played works by Bach, Brahms, Debussy, Poulenc, Bartok and Grieg.

Sam Baker gave an organ recital on Friday 18 August at midday, and S. Chad's Choir sang Choral Evensong at 6.00pm, which included Psalms 93 and 94, Moeran in D and Elgar's 'Light of the World'. That day's music concluded with a concert by Shrewsbury Chamber Singers and Orchestra at 8.00pm.

Saturday 19 August began with an organ recital at midday by Dr Caleb Jarvis, Sam's boyhood friend, now City Organist of Liverpool. This was followed by The London Chorale under the direction of Simon Preston (with Sam Baker organ) singing Evensong at 4.00pm. The music included Psalms 98, 99, 100 and 101; Byrd's Great Service and Parsons' 'Ave Maria'. They then sang a Solemn Eucharist at 6.00pm with music by Palestrina, Brahms, Bruckner and Rachmaninov.

The dedication of the church was celebrated on Sunday 20 August with choral services sung by S. Chad's Choir. The music for the morning mass was a setting in G by Clifford Harker and for Evensong included Psalm 48, Stanford in C, 'Let the bright seraphim' and 'Let their celestial concerts all unite' by Handel.

The Choir's repertoire increased slowly throughout this time and they began to undertake trips to sing at other notable venues. Lichfield and Hereford Cathedrals and Leominster Priory were of particular note, but regular visits were made to the Chapel at Little Berwick on the Berwick Estate, and to S. Eata's, Atcham, both places where there were personal links of one kind or another. Visiting choirs also came to S. Chad's to sing on many occasions. One such example is the Buxton Madrigal Singers singing Choral Evensong for the Epiphany on Saturday 6 January 1973 at 5.00pm. After Choral Evensong on Passion Sunday (8 April) 1973 the combined choirs and orchestras of Adams Grammar School Newport and the Priory Girls' Grammar School performed Berlioz's 'Te Deum'.

In 1973 an alternative festival was celebrated in July and included events in both S. Chad's and S. Mary's. S. Chad's hosted another exhibition of paintings, sculpture, embroidery and ceramics, and S. Mary's hosted a Flower Festival. Events included: music by the Phoenix Singers of Shrewsbury with the Stretton Dancers and the Shropshire County Youth Orchestra conducted by Richard White; a Combined Sunday morning High Mass at S. Mary's at which the preacher was the Bishop of Lichfield, Dr Stretton Reeve; Solemn Evensong in S. Chad's at which the preacher was the Reverend John Ginever, Rector of Wolverhampton; a staging of T S Eliot's 'Murder in the Cathedral' by the Abbey Foregate Players; a performance of Haydn's 'Nelson Mass' by the Shrewsbury Chamber Singers; a concert by the S. Cecilia Singers of Chester, conducted by Ronald Hugh Smith; an evening of Baroque Trio Sonatas, performed by Hamish Drummond (violin), Philip Lewis (flute), Judith Horner (cello) and Sam Baker (piano); and a High Mass held by the Guild of the Servants of the Sanctuary, at which the preacher was the Right Reverend Francis Cocks, Bishop of Shrewsbury. Several other Evensongs were sung by S. Chad's Choir over the days of the Festival (either the full choir or boys voices only) and the Festival ended with a concert given by Shrewsbury Symphony Orchestra.

Although this July festival replaced the usual music during the Flower Show, The London Chorale under the direction of Simon Preston again returned to S. Chad's to give concerts on Saturday 11 August 1973 and in August 1974, at which Sam Baker also played organ solos. He also performed one of the opening recitals on the newly restored organ in Lichfield Cathedral on Sunday 4 August 1974 at 8.00pm.

The 1975 Flower Show musical programme was a little more restricted and included an organ concert by Sam Baker on Friday 15 August at midday and S. Chad's Choir singing Choral Evensong with music by Barnby and Vaughan Williams. On Saturday 16 August the church choir sang Choral Evensong with music by Walmisley and Handel, and that evening, one of Sam's pupils, David Leeke, gave an organ recital at 7.00pm.

Simon Preston again returned with the London Chorale on Saturday 13 September 1975 to sing Evensong at 5.45pm and a concert at 7.00pm which was broadcast on BBC radio. The concert featured motets by Taverner, Gibbons and Weelkes; 'Jesu priceless treasure' by Bach; madrigals and songs by Wilbye, Stanford and Grainger; organ solos played by Sam Baker; and a horn quartet by Rimsky-Korsakov, performed by Julian Baker, Peter Smith, Colin Horton and Peter Civil (cousin of famous horn player, Alan Civil). The other horn pieces in this concert were a Sea Shanty by Lowell

Shaw, and Mozart's 'Ave Verum Corpus'. Julian recalls: "I looked up in the middle of that and saw Dad grinning broadly, because, as he said afterwards, it was so strange - i.e. 'wrong' - to hear it performed in G major!"

On Saturday 4 October 1975 the Esterhazy Singers gave a concert of music by Schütz and Buxtehude, Psalm 100 (Jauchzet dem Herrn) by Mendelssohn and Psalm 117 (Laudate Jehovam) by Telemann.

S. Chad's continued to host many of the county's 'state' occasions: weddings, funerals and memorial services, as well as services attended by the Judiciary for the start of each session of the Crown Court. One such, held on the penultimate day of Sam Baker's time in office, Saturday 18 September 1975, was a service of thanksgiving for the life of Sir Offley Wakeman, Bart. The service, conducted by the Vicar, the Reverend Christopher Spafford, had contributions from the Chairman of the County Council, Lieutenant Colonel R C G Morris-Eyton, and the Right Reverend Arthur Partridge, Assistant Bishop of Hereford, as well as The Right Reverend Francis Cocks, Bishop of Shrewsbury. The sermon was preached by the Right Reverend Stretton Reeve, the former Bishop of Lichfield. According to the service sheet the congregation stood for a solemn Te Deum (Boyce in A) at the end of the service sung by the church choir. Dr Stretton Reeve had, in S. Chad's on Advent Sunday 1974, preached his last sermon to the diocese as its bishop. From here he took leave of his post, and this also indicated the status in which S. Chad's was held within the diocese. The music was significant and the liturgy creative: part the office of Evensong, part a 'service of light' for Advent combined with this important sermon.

The service of thanksgiving for Sir Offley Wakeman was followed by a choir party hosted in the vicarage by Christopher and Stephanie Spafford to mark the retirement of Sam Baker after a memorable incumbency in charge of S. Chad's music. Sam retired on Sunday 19 October, 1975 after a feast of music at all the services. His successor was to be Richard Stephens, Director of Music at The Priory Boys' Grammar School and Conductor of the Concord Singers.

An excellent relationship and friendship existed between vicar and organist during the time of Christopher Spafford and Sam Baker. The archives contain a note from vicar to organist which demonstrates well that clear respect that the one had for the other:

S. Chad's Vicarage
4 July 1975

Dear Sam
With regard to the confirmation; we are having a final preparation on Sunday 13 July at Evensong. The form of service will be just as usual up to the end of the collects and anthem (except that we shall go from 'O Lord, open thou our lips'. ...the remainder of the service will be a preparation and will involve parts being taken by the candidates including a hymn of their choice...

At the Confirmation (7.30pm Wednesday 16 July) I would be really glad if the choir could sing a suitable anthem during the communion and if you would choose some suitable hymns for then also. Please let me know soon what you are going to have. I suggest we have your tune, which Robert [Willis… curate 1972-75] called Oak Street. [This is in fact the tune 'Foremarke' but Robert called it Oak Street after the street in which Sam lived!]
Can we also have 'O thou who camest from above' and 'Come thou holy spirit, come' and 'Praise my soul' as that will be well-known. We must use the A&M words, which are not always the same as those in the English Hymnal.

Please may I have any musical settings which the Bishop is required to sing.

Best wishes
Christopher

A letter also appeared in the monthly newsletter of November 1975:

S. Chad's Vicarage
8 October 1975

My dear friends
Mr Sam Baker announced his intention to retire too late for anything to be written in last month's issue. He has been with us as Organist and Choirmaster for only something over four years, but both he and his wife, Evelyn, have become very dear friends to so many at S. Chad's (many of whom have known him all the years he was at S. Mary's) that their departure comes as a most unhappy shock. He has done wonders with the Choir and on the Organ and has enticed many singers and musicians of great ability to come and delight us. Wales is not exactly the back of beyond so we shall often hope to see them both, to hear him play, bringing some of his wide circle of talented friends with him. Having Sam here has given us a stake in Richard and Julian (three for the price of one!) We certainly hope to keep that stake in all three.

We are very fortunate in finding a worthy successor to Sam Baker in Mr Richard Stephens, Director of Music at the Priory Boys' Grammar School.

Yours very sincerely
Christopher Spafford

S. Chad's was fortunate enough to retain two curates until the middle 1970s and one such had a greater impact on the musical life of the church and town than most. Robert Willis who arrived as a newly ordained deacon in the summer of 1972 was to be heavily involved in the music of S. Chad's during his time as curate. He was the driving force behind the choir's trip to sing at Portsmouth Cathedral for a week in 1973 and numerous other outings were masterminded by him. He was also an accomplished pianist and accompanied the local choral society on many occasions, as well as starting to put pen to paper as a hymn writer. Robert left S. Chad's to become the Succentor of Salisbury Cathedral in 1975. In retirement, Sam Baker began assisting on occasions at S. David's Cathedral, and he reported back to S. Chad's the following notice seen there: "*This is the House of God. Please refrain from eating ice cream and smoking. Leave your pets outside.*" 1975's carol service (held on 30 December as carols were not encouraged in Advent) was memorable: it was the first under the direction of Richard Stephens and the music was particularly well-presented. Richard Stephens was a fine player who gave a number of organ recitals in his time at S. Chad's, and also conducted both The Concord Singers and The Tudor Singers.

Richard Stephens directed the Requiem by Duruflé on Saturday 22 November 1975 (S. Cecilia's Day – the Patron of Music and Musicians). He also presented a concert in November, sung by The Concord Singers, accompanied by Roger Parkes (Organist of Shrewsbury School). This concert included Buxtehude's 'Magnificat'; Bach's Cantata 106 'Actus tragicus-Gottes Zeit'; Partita for Organ by William Mathias', and ended with Britten's 'Rejoice in the Lamb'. Other concerts that year included The Cantanti Camerati of Richmond on Saturday 6 December, and the Priory Boys' Grammar School Choir and Orchestra performing Handel's 'Messiah' on Monday 8 December.

The Flower Show music in 1976 was arranged by David Leeke (who subsequently arranged this each year until 2002) as Richard Stephens was giving organ recitals in the USA at that time. The London Chorale again returned to S. Chad's on Saturday 4 September 1976, this time conducted by Godfrey Salmons with John Langdon (organ). They sang music by Taverner, Weelkes, Gibbons, Ireland, Britten and Howells. The Vicar, Christopher Spafford left S. Chad's on Sunday 12 September 1976 and was instituted as Provost (Dean) of Newcastle Cathedral on Saturday 2 October at 3.00pm.
The interregnum was led by The Reverend Peter Smith, the Senior Curate who wrote in the November Newsletter about music:

S. Chad's has always been a favourite venue for musical events because of its splendid acoustics, its large seating capacity and the beauty of the setting in which one can enjoy the music of the masters. Since Richard Stephens' appointment as Organist and Choirmaster we have been able to set up a special arts Sub-Committee of the Church Council, and they have been busy drawing up an exciting programme of concerts for the year ahead. Perhaps it will help if we set out the programme in the form of a concert diary, so that you can make a note of those events which appeal to you. We hope there will be something for all tastes!

1976

November 10	*The Aeolian String Quartet – internationally famous, seen recently in a series on television. A programme of works by Mozart, Beethoven and Panufnik.*
December 5	*Rolls Royce Male Voice Choir – a Sunday evening concert.*
December 15	*'Messiah' – sung by Shrewsbury Choral Society.*

January 12	*The Fitzwilliam String Quartet – an outstanding Quartet in a programme of works by Mozart, Shostakovich and Sibelius.*
January 19	*Dvorak Mass in D and Kodaly Missa Brevis – sung by Shrewsbury Choral Society.*
February 10	*Carol Brown (flute). A recital by the very talented Shrewsbury girl who is now studying at the Royal Academy of Music in London.*
March (tbc)	*A Young People's Concert organised by Mr David Grundy.*
April 23	*The Esterhazy Singers and Orchestra – a programme to include motets by Bach, a Haydn Mass and works by Buxtehude.*
May 18	*Verdi's Requiem – sung by Shrewsbury Choral Society*
May 31	*Mozart's Requiem – sung by the Choir of the Priory Boys' Grammar School.*
June 22	*Midsummer Concert – presented by Shrewsbury Symphony Orchestra.*
July 9	*Gary Karr (double bass) – internationally celebrated virtuoso of the double bass.*

In addition to these concerts we are hoping to arrange a concert by the London Woodwind Quintet in May and another recital by Joanne Cohen (violin) and Roger Parkes (piano) in April.

Theatre lovers are not being neglected in this splendid series of live performances because we hope that Theatre Roundabout will pay a return visit to S. Chad's next May. I hope you will be able to attend them.

We are fortunate to have such an enthusiastic group of people on the Arts Sub-Committee to plan and arrange this splendid programme for us and we owe a tremendous debt of gratitude to Mrs Joy Charlesworth for her gift to the church of the beautiful piano, which has replaced the one formerly on loan from Mr Sam Baker. It is a most wonderful gesture, and it will be such an asset for any musical events we arrange in church.

[NB this piano is now to be found in S. Chad's sister church, S. Alkmund's]

The induction of the next Vicar, The Reverend Michael Pollit, took place on Thursday 16 December 1976 at 7.30pm and was followed by a reception in the Priory Boys' Grammar School.

The centenary of the robed voluntary choir took place in 1977 and was marked by a Choral Evensong on Friday 15 July at 7.45pm. For the occasion, S. Chad's Choir sang: Psalms 122 and 150; Harris 'Behold the tabernacle of God'; Brewer in D and Statham's anthem 'Praise thou the Lord O my soul'. This was followed by a dinner at which the guest speaker was Sam Baker. In a busy month for the choir, they had also recently sung at a national service for the centenary of the S. John Ambulance Brigade and at a regular Crown Court Service.

The July 1977 edition of *Shropshire Magazine* contained an article about the choir at S. Chad's: Ralph Oldham visited the church to attend a choir practice where he "*admired the sweetness of tone of the men and boys as they rehearsed*". He and a colleague, Tom [surname not known], viewed the documents appertaining to the foundation of the present choir in 1877 and noted the rules from that time suggesting that they were regarded a century on as "*quite severe*". The article continued: "*I formed an impression of complete devotion to duty on the part of the boys we met the other evening! At Christmas they and the men take part in many carol services not only in their own church but in various village churches, as well as the nearby Ear Nose and Throat Hospital. On Good Friday morning the men sing the Passion according to S. John to plainsong during the Eucharist and Veneration of the Cross. Evensong is also sung to plainsong. Easter Eve and Easter Day are fully honoured in music, culminating with Choral Evensong. On Ascension Day the choir observes the picturesque tradition of climbing onto the church roof at half past six in the morning to sing appropriate hymns after which there is a Choral Eucharist. Approximately four times a year the choir takes part in a special service attended by the Crown Court Judge, and at Flower Show time musical services are held for the benefit of visitors.*

Among the places outside the county where the choir has sung are Lichfield and Hereford Cathedrals and Leominster Priory. In 1973 under their former Master of Choristers, Samuel Baker, they sang the services for a week at Portsmouth Cathedral. Mr Baker will be guest of honour at a centenary dinner for the men following Festal Evensong on Friday 15 July…The boys will have a special outing a few days later. On July 21 [BBC TV] 'Songs of Praise' will be recorded at S. Chad's, and the probable date for its transmission is December 11.

The choir have certainly ended their first century in very fine form, and I am sure that as they enter their second they will have the very best wishes of all fellow choristers and music-lovers throughout Shropshire."

The world virtuoso double bass player, Gary Karr gave a memorable concert on his priceless instrument dating from 1611. The then Vicar, Michael Pollit, has said recently: "*For me probably the most memorable concert I've ever been privileged to listen to was Gary Karr's (with Harman Lewis on the organ) on 9 July, 1977. He was regarded as the world's No 1 virtuoso on the double bass. It was simply 'spine shivering' stuff! At the Eucharist on Sunday 10 July he played from the gallery during the administration of communion. I think all of us felt we were in heaven (which we were I suppose). (I think it was Bruch's 'Kol Nidrei' he was playing). When 'Down Your Way' came to Shrewsbury & I was interviewed in S. Chad's by the cricket commentator, Brian Johnson, I chose for my piece of music the Kol Nidrei version played by Gary. It was on the disc Gary presented to me which I had to lend to the BBC because their record library hadn't got a recording!*"

The Flower Show music of 1977 had the usual Evensongs sung by the church choir. There were also organ recitals by David Leeke, Richard Pilliner, who had been a chorister at S. Chad's (1971-1976) and was then studying at the Royal Academy of Music, and Andrew Lucas, who also went to school in Shrewsbury and was then studying at the Royal College of Music.

Richard Stephens took up a new teaching post and was succeeded as Organist and Choirmaster by David Grundy, who was then Director of Music at the Wakeman Grammar School. One of David Grundy's first undertakings in his new role was to direct the choir at Lichfield Cathedral at Choral

Evensong on Sunday 21 August. The male choir was maintained by him for the next four years and some memorable trips to sing at major venues were undertaken, perhaps especially to Liverpool Anglican and RC Cathedrals. Generally the Grundy years are remembered for their small increase in active congregational participation in the music of the services. This may have been in vogue at many churches at the time, and was probably thought of as the norm, but here it resonated strongly with the particular tastes and personality of David Grundy, who was anxious to remove any whiff of what he regarded as the elitism of cathedral-style worship.

On 17 March 1978 S. Chad's hosted a concert given by The Academy of Ancient Music, and on 13 July that year the Selwyn Centenary Service was held in S. Chad's. Michael Pollit again writes: "*One of the most memorable services at S. Chad's was the Selwyn Centenary Service on 13th July 1978 when the Archbishop of Melanesia preached and ALL the Diocesan Bishops and staff were present (about 800 in church). I believe it was the first time we had invited the Stretton School of Dance and Drama to participate, under the direction of the brilliant Diana Griffiths. She was a great teacher and exponent of Classical Greek Dance and an expert choreographer. We were privileged on many occasions to welcome them to S. Chad's to participate in our worship. They made a very special contribution to the services for the MENCAP and the Deaf Church. They were SO professional and made Liturgical Dance, for me at least, a significant element in worship.*"

In 1978 the Flower Show programme remained rather similar to the previous year, with recitals by Murray Stewart, David Leeke, Peter Newell (later, for many years, Organist of Ashford Parish Church, Kent) and Richard Pilliner who also accompanied the Festival Chorus in a concert of choral music on Saturday 12 August at 8.00pm.

For the 1979 Flower Show, as well as the usual Evensongs, Richard Pilliner gave an organ recital on Friday 10 August at midday, Roy Woodhams (Organist of S. John's, Margate) played at 3.00pm and the day concluded with a concert of organ and piano music presented by David Leeke and Janice Phillimore. On Saturday 11 August, Peter Newell gave an organ recital and Richard Pilliner gave an organ and vocal concert with soprano Julie Hunter. The Festival Chorus gave a concert of church anthems conducted by David Leeke with Richard Pilliner (organ).

In January 1980 David Grundy wrote an interesting article on church music in the church Newsletter.

In a recent edition of 'Church Music', the quarterly magazine published by the Royal School of Church Music, there are some forthright utterances by a number of eminent church musicians on organists, clergy and the state of church music in general.

"*Where is the musical conscience of the organist and/or choirmaster who suffocates the spirit of music as a weekly ritual? I offer thanks to the church musician who does the job well; I offer nothing but anger to the man who destroys music through no fault of his own.*" [Basil Ramsey in Organists' Review, August 1978]
The Director of the RSCM, Lionel Dakers, asserts that despite the "successful outreach of the RSCM…good music at ordinary church level is becoming more of a rarity…"

The term "good music" needn't imply elaborate cathedral-style settings sung in front of a mute congregation; Mr Dakers points the finger at the organist, whose playing is often unhelpful, unrhythmic and utterly hostile to the cause of good singing choral and congregational. "The harm done by such people (to worship) is much greater than we realise…Many of the culprits are unwilling to take any action simply because they cannot, or will not, recognise their faults. In the highly competitive business world…such attitudes and standards would never for a moment be tolerated, yet in church second best, or even the mediocre, is readily accepted." Worse, "there is the disquieting knowledge that so many are opting out of church music determined not to go back into it." Mr Dakers goes on to ask why this should be, examining conditions of work and the attitude of some clergy.

This is a very complex matter and somewhat diffidently I offer the following observations, confining myself on this occasion to practical matters.

Many church organists do give faithful service, week in and week out up and down the country. A small number – not necessarily professionals – reach a high standard and occasionally there might be a bank manager, say, with an organist's diploma, but many are complacent, amateurish, content with a low standard of execution and sometimes blissfully unaware of their deficiencies. It is not expected that every organist give brilliant performances of difficult organ recital works – the state of many instruments would preclude this anyway – but it should be possible for such a person to be able to play hymns adequately. For this there are certain vital basic requirements:

- *That the organist play a hymn so that the congregation can recognise the tune.*
- *That the performance shall be* **rhythmic.** *Rhythm in all music is of prime importance, not a soulless metronomic beat, but a regular rhythmic pulse. To find this in church is exceptional. Why don't vast numbers of organists – faithful though they no doubt are – seek professional advice? Why must they indulge in such irritating mannerisms, like hanging on to the last chord after the singing has finished, and worse, releasing the chord note by note? Or reducing the organ to a whisper when the word "death" crops up in a hymn for example, " and may the music of Thy name refresh my soul (quieter and slower) in death"?*

Possibly the worst sin of all is the widespread habit of playing the introduction to a hymn at one speed, and then beginning the actual singing at another. Many facts govern the pace at which hymns should be sung, acoustics of the building, size of congregation and so on, but the main factor is the character of the hymn to be sung, and this should be understood by the organist. But please, above all, let us have consistent rhythm and a sense of flow! If the Vicar will allow me, I might refer to this topic again in the future.

David Grundy

There seems to be no evidence in print that David Grundy did, in fact, return to this topic.

The Flower Show music continued in much the same vein: 1980 saw more recitals from many of those already mentioned plus Gary Cole (later to run Regent Records). Sam Baker died during the 1980

Flower Show Music Festival on Sunday 17 August; David Leeke played for his funeral at S. Dogmael's Parish Church where he is buried in the churchyard. Later that year, on All Saints' Day, Saturday 1 November 1980, a memorial service was held at S. Chad's. Another of Sam's former pupils, the late George Guest played the organ. Before the service he played:

Pazienza	Whitlock
Rhosymedre	Vaughan Williams
Psalm Prelude Set 1, Number 1	Howells
Chorale Prelude on Schmücke dich	J S Bach

The choir sang Harris' 'Behold the tabernacle of God' and Wood's 'O Thou the central orb'.
The lesson was read by Michael Charlesworth, OBE who was Second Master of Shrewsbury School and the address was given by Robert Glover, Sam's Headmaster at Adams' Grammar School, Newport, and father of another of Sam's pupils, the Conductor and Musicologist, Dr Jane Glover. The service concluded with George Guest playing Bach's 'S. Anne Fugue'.

1981 was thus a memorial festival to Sam, in which Caroline Trevor sang the Song Cycle 'Let us garlands bring' as a tribute to both Sam and the 80th anniversary of the birth of Finzi. The Festival Chorus also sang the Requiem by Fauré in memory of Sam. This concert, conducted by David Leeke, was attended by many of the good and great of the musical fraternity, including a number of cathedral organists.

In this era, secondary education in Shropshire was re-organised, and as a result David Grundy became Director of Music at the new Shrewsbury Sixth Form College. Pressures of work resulted in his relinquishing the post as Organist and Choirmaster in 1981, and he was succeeded by Roger Allen. Having moved to Shrewsbury for the job at St Chad's, Roger also took on work at Prestfelde Preparatory School. This aided him in his first task, which was immediately recruiting more boys for the treble line. Under Roger Allen the choir thrived and many important standard works to the repertoire were added. Perhaps significantly a fine rendering of Allegri's 'Miserere' was remembered by many when the treble soloist was Guy Booth who went on to have a sparkling musical career with army bands. Roger Allen's sixth-form pupil from his days at Ellesmere College, Roger Muttitt, began to undertake more of the accompanying, allowing Roger Allen to direct the music from downstairs. Roger Muttitt went on to read music at the University of Hull, during which time he was Organ Scholar of both the University and Beverley Minster, before undertaking post graduate study at the Royal Academy of Music and the post of Organ Scholar at S. George's Chapel, Windsor. He subsequently embarked upon a teaching career. David Grundy remained a member of S. Chad's and often sang in the choir.

Michael Pollit celebrated his Silver Jubilee as a priest in 1982 with a Choral Eucharist sung by the church choir which included the singing of 'I was glad' by Parry. The preacher then was The Venerable Charles Borrett, Archdeacon of Stoke-on-Trent.

Simon Lole, Adrian Williams and Christopher Muhley performed at the 1982 Flower Show Festival and Lionel Bourne, David Leeke, Roy Woodhams and Adrian Williams played at the 1983 Festival.

S. Chad's role as 'county church' was again cemented with the funeral of Viscount Bridgeman, the Lord Lieutenant of Shropshire in December 1982. Roger Allen directed the music at the service and the choir sang the anthem by S S Wesley 'Who can express the noble acts of the Lord'. The Bishop of Hereford, the Right Reverend John Eastaugh gave the address.

The church continued (as it does today) to host many of the local musical societies' concerts; one such was a performance of Elgar's 'Dream of Gerontius' sung by Shrewsbury Choral Society under the direction of David Grundy on Saturday 26 March 1983. Soloists were Joyce Ellis (soprano), James Griffett (tenor), Christopher Underwood (bass) and the semi-chorus was the choir of S. Chad's, by then under the direction of Roger Allen. The orchestra on that occasion was led by Peter Lewis.

In the late spring of 1983 an appeal was launched for the restoration of the tower and the rehabilitation of the organ. Nicholson's action of 1963 did not stand up to the heavy wear and tear to which any organ in S. Chad's is subjected, so, at a cost of £31,000, Harrison and Harrison of Durham were engaged to sort out the difficulties with the action. This work was undertaken in 1984-1985 by which time Roger Allen had moved on, and the new Organist and Choirmaster was Marc Rochester. At the same time, Harrison's carried out the wishes of Roger Allen in making some tonal adjustments to the instrument: the Octave (wood) and four-foot Flute on the pedals were replaced with a Principal (metal) and Fifteenth respectively.

The restoration of the organ was celebrated with a Choral Evensong for S. Chad's day on Sunday 3 March 1985, after which Jonathan Rees-Williams, Organist of Lichfield Cathedral, gave a thrilling demonstration of the restored organ's capabilities. The Newsletter of April 1985 records: "*Those not at this service may like to know that more than £10,000 [of the £31,000 raised] was given in memory of Sam Baker, well-remembered and much loved organist at S. Chad's, and a prominent figure in the musical life of Shropshire. It was fitting that Mrs Baker and her son, Richard, were able to be present at the Thanksgiving Evensong and Recital.*"

Formed in 1984, The Shropshire Music Trust gave its first series of concerts at S. Chad's in 1984-1985. Although they did not return to S. Chad's after this for some fifteen years, S. Chad's has been delighted to host several of the Shropshire Music Trust's many concerts since then. A list of these concerts can be found in Appendix 3. One of the regular contributors to the Shropshire Music Trust programme over many years has been Ex Cathedra, who originally performed a Christmas event in S. Mary's. However, since 2000 the numbers attending outgrew S. Mary's and 'Christmas by Candlelight' has now become an annual and much loved part of Christmas celebrations at S. Chad's.

Between 1984 and 2002, the church choir was used rather less at the Flower Show, and most of the services were sung by the Festival Choir, drawn from all over the country. The curate of the early 1980s, The Reverend Philip Chester, organised many parties and social occasions for these musicians. Notable musical highlights from these years include: Roger Muttitt's performance in the 1985 Festival which celebrated the tercentenaries of Bach, Handel and Domenico Scarlatti; the Preacher on the Sunday at the Festival Eucharist that same year, The Reverend Canon Peter Cole, Vicar of Folkestone; the 1987 Festival Choir concerts of Elgar's 'Give unto the Lord' and Parry's 'Blest Pair of Sirens' as well as 'Ascribe unto the Lord' by S S Wesley and a concert version of 'Acis and Galatea' by Handel; the 1988 performance of Dvorak's 'Mass in D'; and the 1990 Festival Choir concert of the music of Elgar. Organ Recitals in 1990 were given by David Leeke and Reg Adams (Organist of Holy Trinity, Broadstairs).

By the 1986 Festival William (Bill) Smallman had become Director of Music at S. Chad's and was happy to be part of the team of recitalists, some of whom are already mentioned above. The New English Hymnal was introduced to S. Chad's as the standard book for all services on Sunday 4 September 1988.

Further tonal alterations were made to the organ in 1990 by Harrison and Harrison. The work was financed by Bill Smallman in memory of his parents. The Nicholson Gemshorn on the choir organ was transposed to a Tierce and the Mixture on the great organ was altered to remove an awkward break, and to sit more comfortably on the Diapason Chorus.

In 1991 The Festival Choir undertook two masses: 'Missa Sancti Joannis de Deo' by Haydn and Mozart's 'Coronation Mass' with local soloists: Joyce Rogers (soprano), Elizabeth Bowring (alto), Brian Clee (tenor) and Bryan Harper (bass).

1992 saw the bicentenary of the building and the 1200th anniversary of the founding of S. Chad's by King Offa. There was a programme of special events throughout the year:

Shrewsbury School Chapel Choir under the direction of Richard Dacey gave a concert at 8.00pm on Sunday 23 February. The Patronal Festival that year was celebrated on Sunday 1 March with the choir singing Haydn's 'Little Organ Mass' with strings, and preacher the Reverend Canon Robert Willis, Vicar of Sherborne Abbey and curate of S. Chad's from 1972-1975 (later Dean of Hereford and Dean of Canterbury). At Choral Evensong that day the Garden of Remembrance was dedicated by the Bishop of Lichfield and the service was attended by the congregations from both the former daughter churches of S. George, Frankwell, and Christ Church, Shelton and Oxon, as well as members of S. Alkmund's.

Many former clergy returned that year and the Holy Week Triduum was led by the Very Reverend Christopher Spafford, Vicar of S. Chad's 1969-1976, and who became Provost of Newcastle. Dr Roy Massey, Organist of Hereford Cathedral gave an organ recital on Tuesday 28 April, as did Jennifer Bate on Wednesday 6 May. Shrewsbury Male Voice choir performed on Saturday 9 May, on Tuesday 12 May the Choir of Lichfield Cathedral gave a concert, and Shrewsbury Symphony Orchestra gave a concert on Tuesday 19 May. An Organ Recital by Jonathan Rees-Williams, who was then just about to move from his post as Organist of Lichfield Cathedral to become Organist of S. George's Chapel, Windsor, was held on Tuesday 26 May.

A procession took place from Old S. Chad's to New S. Chad's on the Feast of Pentecost at which the preacher at the mass in the present church was the Reverend Canon Geoffrey Bostock, Vicar of Bilham, Doncaster and a former curate. The Reverend Canon Paul Lucas, Precentor of Wells Cathedral, and a former Chaplain of Shrewsbury School also returned to preach, and Harry Bramma, Director of the RSCM conducted a local choirs festival on Saturday 20 June. Howard Franklin presented a gala evening with flowers, music and verse on Tuesday 30 June and during that month there were organ recitals from Bill Smallman (Tuesday 9), Paul Derrett, at that time Organist of Christ Church, Cheltenham (Saturday 13), and Andrew Lucas, then Sub Organist of S. Paul's Cathedral (Tuesday 23). Frank Shelton brought over his choir from Colorado Springs, USA to sing a US Episcopal Rite Mass on Sunday 5 July, and he gave an organ recital on Saturday 4 July. Also in July the Right Reverend Graham Leonard, KCVO, former Bishop of London preached at a High Mass. Further recitals were given on Tuesday 14 July (Hugh Davies of S. Asaph Cathedral) and Tuesday 28 July (Michael Rhodes of Stoke on Trent).

The regular recitalists returned once again for the Flower Show music festival and the Festival Choir under the direction of David Leeke sang Vivaldi's 'Gloria' and 'Five Mystical Songs'. by Vaughan Williams Organ Recitals were given by Reg Adams (Holy Trinity, Broadstairs) and Roy Woodhams (then in training for the Anglican Priesthood and Director of Music at Ripon College, Cuddesdon).

The music for Choral Evensong that day was all by Herbert Howells, the centenary of whose birth was in 1992, and the choir presented a celebration in words and music at 8.00pm that evening. The conductor was David Leeke, Roger Muttitt played the organ, and poems were read by Dick Tanswell, a member of the church congregation.

The preacher at the Festival Eucharist (sung to Schubert in G) was the Right Reverend Ronnie Bowlby, the retired Bishop of Southwark, (who retired to Shrewsbury to become a member of S. Chad's congregation and an Honorary Assistant Priest on the staff of S. Chad's!) The preacher at Evensong was the Reverend Canon Peter Cole, Rural Dean of Alton, Hampshire. Compline was sung to plainsong in memory of Sam Baker on Monday 17 August (12 years to the day after his death) and this was followed by a memorial organ recital by David Leeke (then Director of Music at Maidstone Grammar School).

On the 200th anniversary of the actual day of consecration, Wednesday 19 August 1992, Choral Communion was celebrated as it might have been in 1792. David Leeke conducted this service and the preacher was The Reverend Christopher Irving, Principal of S. Stephen's House, Oxford. This service began at the church door when the choir sang Bruckner's 'Locus iste' (not actually written in 1792!) and then after prayers of penitence in the vestibule the entire procession moved into the church singing the hymn 'Lift high the Cross'. Although the liturgy was probably fairly authentic, the music and hymns were clearly not: a commissioned piece 'Christ is our cornerstone' by David Grundy received its premiere at this service!

Roger Fisher, Organist of Chester Cathedral gave an organ recital on Tuesday 25 August. On Tuesday 8 September there was a High Mass for the Blessed Virgin Mary, at which the preacher was The Reverend Roy Fellows, Guardian of the Shrine of Walsingham, and this was followed by a Flower Festival with musical items from Friday 11 – Sunday 13 September. The Preacher on this day (also Battle of Britain Sunday) was the Right Reverend Peter Ball, Bishop of Gloucester. Richard Pilliner (then organist of S. Matthew's, Croydon) returned to give an organ recital on Tuesday 22 September and Harvest Choral Evensong had as its preacher the Reverend Canon Donald Gray, Canon of Westminster, Rector of S. Margaret's, Westminster and Chaplain to the Speaker of the House of Commons. The New English Orchestra and Singers under their conductor, Nigel Swinford, gave a concert on Saturday 3 October and took part in further dedication liturgy on Sunday 4 October, when the preacher was the Reverend David Allcock, Chaplain of Shrewsbury School and a former curate. Bill Smallman gave a recital on Tuesday 6 October. November saw various special services: the Bishop of Shrewsbury confirmed on All Saints' Day and the preacher at the Civic Service of Remembrance was the Reverend Robert Pyne, a naval chaplain who had grown up as a server at S. Chad's twenty or so years earlier. The year ended with a concert in December by Shrewsbury Choral Society conducted by David Grundy: The Requiem Mass by Duruflé and the S. Cecilia Mass by Gounod.

After the excitement of the bicentenary, 1993 was a quieter year. The Flower Show Music Festival continued and there were recitals by David Leeke, Bill Smallman and David Grundy, and a Festival concert included a Bach Cantata. On Friday 13 August there was a concert of light music for a summer's evening which included part songs, madrigals and songs from World War II as well as poetry presented by Dick Tanswell. Dr Philip Pettit (recently retired Headmaster of Maidstone Grammar School) visited the church on Sunday 15 August 1993 to present an act of worship exploring the history, and some of the trends and styles of hymnody, used in English churches of all traditions.

The 1994 Flower Show Festival continued in the same vein: organ recitals were given by Alistair Berwick (S. Mary's, Kemsing, Sevenoaks), David Grundy and Roger Muttitt (Director of Music at Durham School) and the Festival Choir sang Bernstein's 'Chichester Psalms', Mendelssohn's 'Hear my prayer', Haydn's 'Insanae et vanae curae' and 'Te Deum' under the direction of David Leeke. The Preacher at the Festival Eucharist was The Reverend John Murray, Assistant Chaplain General to the Forces.

The Flower Show Festival of 1995 saw organ recitals by Peter Kirk (All Souls', Cheriton, Folkestone), Simon Lole (then Organist of Sheffield Cathedral), and Roger Muttitt, and the Festival Choir sang a concert version of Purcell's 'Dido and Aeneas'.

By the 1996 Festival, S. Chad's had a new Vicar: The Reverend Christopher Liley (later Archdeacon of Lichfield). Recitals and Evensongs continued as before, organists coming to play included Reg Adams, Roy Woodhams (by now Priest in Charge of Sholden, Deal, Kent), David Leeke and Robert Fuller (then Assistant Director of Music at Maidstone Grammar School). That year David Leeke conducted the Festival Chorus in a performance of Handel's 'Ode on S. Cecilia's Day' with William Hayward (Shrewsbury Abbey) accompanying on the organ.

In 1997, the Vicar sought to change the established pattern of the Flower Show Music Festival, by having musical interludes on the hour from 10.00am to 4.00pm with Choral Evensong each day at 5.00pm; the Festival Concert (English Church Music through the centuries, conducted by David Leeke) was held in place of Evensong on Sunday 17 August. This pattern was repeated during the incumbency of Chris Liley as Vicar, and in 1998 and David Leeke brought a number of his pupils (or ex-pupils) from Maidstone Grammar School to add variety. These included Nicola Corbishley (later a significant London-based singer), Robert Simmons (later a violinist in the Orchestra of the Royal Opera House, Covent Garden), as well as contributions from Reg Adams, David Grundy, Roy Woodhams and Robert Fuller. The Festival concert in 1998 was immediately after the morning Eucharist (at which the ordinary of the mass was by Reg Adams) and was conducted by David Leeke with Reg Adams playing the organ. 1997 was a celebration of the life of Sir Hubert Parry and featured three of his choral pieces, 'I was glad', 'My soul, there is a country' (from the Songs of Farewell) and 'Blest Pair of Sirens'. In 1999 yet more of David Leeke's former pupils joined in the musical interludes: Nathan Cline and James Olley to name but two, and in addition to those who had been coming to this festival for years, Jean Bourne and David and Leonie Saint also made solo contributions. The Festival Eucharist on Sunday 15 August was sung to the Mass for Four Voices by Byrd and The Festival Chorus performed parts of Handel's 'Messiah' on Sunday 15 August at 11.30am. In 2000 Jean Bourne (voice), Roy Woodhams (organ),

David Grundy (organ), Leonie Saint (voice), Nathan Cline and James Olley (vocal duo), Anne Hanney (voice), Emma Pierce (voice), Rachel Simmons (oboe), Gillian Dainty (cello) and Robert Simmons (violin) all provided musical interludes and the Festival Chorus performed Vivaldi's 'Gloria'.

The Reverend Christopher Liley had moved by the Flower Show Festival in 2001 and so the pattern again changed. Dino Rizzo, a distinguished Italian organist opened the proceedings with a recital at 1.00pm on Friday 10 August. Robert Simmons gave a violin recital with Robert Fuller, piano at 3.00pm and Choral Evensong was sung at 5.00pm to Sumsion in G with the anthem 'Cantique de Jean Racine' by Fauré. On Saturday 11 August the 1.00pm recital was by Leonie Saint (alto) with Robert Fuller (piano), Nicola Corbishley (soprano) with Robert Fuller (piano) and an organ solo by David Grundy. The 3.00pm recital was by Emma Pierce (soprano) with David Grundy (piano), Nick Bland (organ), and Nathan Cline (euphonium) with Robert Fuller (piano). Choral Evensong was at 5.00pm and included music by Noble and Bairstow. Later that year, David Leeke gave an organ recital in S. Chad's on Friday 14 September of music by Grayston Ives, Saint Saens, Rheinberger, Whitlock and Sidney Campbell.

By 2002 S. Chad's had yet another new Vicar, The Reverend Mark Thomas. Mark, like a number of his predecessors, had come from Yorkshire the previous year. In 2002 David Leeke relinquished the arranging of the Flower Show music after 26 years in this post, but little did he realise that in only a few years time he would be Director of Music at S. Chad's and hence back in this role! On Friday 16 August there were vocal recitals by Leonie Saint with Robert Fuller (piano) and Jean Bourne with David Leeke (piano); and 'musical musings' with James Olley, Erica Phillips and Nathan Cline. On Saturday 17 August there were concerts by Robert Simmons and Susannah Lloyd (violins) with Rachel Simmons (oboe) and Robert Fuller (piano) and the Festival Choir concert was the Requiem by Fauré with Parry's 'Blest pair of Sirens', accompanied by Richard Stephens on the organ. Evensongs were sung both days with music by Brewer, Wood, Bairstow and Noble and the Sunday Eucharist was sung to the 'Little Organ Mass' by Haydn. For this last service of 26 years of these festivals, David Leeke played the organ and David Grundy conducted.

A taste of some of the other musical events held in S. Chad's in 2002 are listed below:

Sunday 18 August	The County Singers sang Choral Evensong at 6.00pm
Sunday 25 August	Concert by 'Quindici' at 3.00pm followed by their singing Choral Evensong
Friday 30 August	Recital by William Hayward (organ) with Wendy Reardon (piano)
Friday 6 September	Organ Recital by Paul Derrett
Friday 20 September	Organ Recital by John Taylor
Saturday 28 September	Organ Recital by Keith Hearnshaw
Friday 4 October	Organ Recital by Bill Smallman
Friday 11 October	Friends of S. Chad's 'Jubilee Delights' concert to celebrate the Golden Jubilee of HM Queen Elizabeth II
Saturday 12 October	Shrewsbury Male Voice Choir
Friday 6 December	Concert of Christmas Music by Ex Cathedra (in candlelight)

Saturday 7 December	Concert by Shrewsbury Choral Society
Saturday 14 December	Concert by the Phoenix Singers
Friday 20 December	Organ Recital by Bill Smallman

The organ's centenary was celebrated in February 2005 with a series of events. This instrument has been criticised for being too loud (unlike its predecessor which was apparently criticised for being too soft, being sited further back in the gallery), but it made its centenary without too much in the way of alteration, so Norman & Beard and Benjamin Pritchard could be regarded as men of vision. Although the church officially seats 1200 people, there have been congregations of 2000 on occasion and this organ has always been voiced to cope with a full church. Its great power comes into its own on Remembrance Sunday and other well-attended Civic Services, when it can make its presence felt even to those good Anglicans who sit as far back as they can under the gallery! It is a little odd, bearing in mind the large number of Civic and 'state' occasions held in S. Chad's, that there has been no powerful reed for fanfares and suchlike. This was to be addressed at the restoration in 2011. Many distinguished organists have played it through the years and by all accounts it is regarded as the most user-friendly instrument in the area.

A series of centenary events were sponsored by:

Arrol and Snell Ltd
Garrards Solicitors
Hatcher Rogerson
The Incorporated Association of Organists
Lanyon Bowdler
The Phoenix Singers of Shrewsbury
The Prince Rupert Hotel, Ltd
Redverse Printers
Shrewsbury Choral Society
Shrewsbury and District Organists' and Choirmasters' Association
Turnbull Garrard
Mr & Mrs R Cooper
Mr V Llewellyn
Mr A Roberts
Mr & Mrs P Williams

An event for schools entitled 'Introduction to the King of Instruments' was held on Thursday 10 February 2005 at 2.00pm, and a masterclass in memory of J Eric Hunt, the founder of the local organists' association was given by Jennifer Bate (Eric Hunt's niece) on Saturday 12 February, 2005. The actual anniversary recital, held exactly 100 years to the day after its opening, was given by Jennifer Bate at 7.30pm on Tuesday 15 February 2005.

By this time the men and boys choir had ceased to exist and initially girls and later adult sopranos were singing the top line. Numbers were low and it was becoming increasingly difficult to maintain the musical tradition of which S. Chad's had been proud for so long. Bill Smallman appended the following to the Organ Centenary brochure:

S. Chad's Choir is always on the lookout for new voices. Hopefully these would match the following criteria:

- A good ear for pitch
- Ability to sight sing
- A blending voice
- Virtually no vibrato
- Ability to get on with people
- A commitment to regular attendance

The choir practises on Fridays beginning at 7.15pm and finishing at 8.30pm. Should there be an influx of youngsters (ages seven to fifteen) the practice for them would begin at 7.00pm and finish at 8.00pm. The choir sings services each Sunday at 9.30am and 6.00pm as its regular commitment. In addition there are several Civic Services each year, plus events such as weddings, funerals, visits to other churches and cathedrals, and the occasional concert. In 2004 the choir has sung at Birmingham, S. Asaph and Lichfield Cathedrals. It seems a lot, but the more singers there are the greater flexibility in attendance.

The repertoire of the choir is largely traditional of what has been called 'Sub-Cathedral' standard, but it does venture into more modern congregational items when needed.

There is also a group of singers who supplement the regular choristers on certain occasions such as a monthly Choral Evensong, Civic and Carol Services. Others provide a choir for the extra services during the period of Shrewsbury Flower Show.

A new innovation is the Junior Singers. These are children of seven and upward who practice for ten minutes after the 9.30am service each Sunday. They prepare a musical item which is performed at the monthly Family Eucharist.

Should you be interested in the foregoing, or require further information, please contact the Director of Music, Bill Smallman.

If you don't match all the criteria, don't worry! The incumbent who appointed the present Director of Music was looking for a married musical archangel, but did not get one! If you match just one condition, you will be welcome!

2005 – 2012

Not much fruit came from this plea although the choir managed in 2005-2006 (Bill Smallman's final year in post) to sing at both Birmingham and S. Asaph Cathedrals. Bill was, however, increasingly unhappy at the rather parlous state of the choir and decided to put in a letter of resignation. So, after twenty-one years he retired in September 2006, the month in which he celebrated his 65th birthday. His final Evensong was followed by a presentation to him and to his wife, Thelma, in the hall. The Vicar, Mark Thomas, asked David Leeke to act as musical adviser in the appointment of Bill's successor. Several people responded to the advert, but, unfortunately, despite a short-list of four being drawn up, only one was available to attend on the day of the interviews. Sue Heath-Downey came with a glittering pedigree and was appointed to start later in the autumn. Unfortunately this incumbency was to be very short; Sue became seriously ill and had to relinquish the post after only six weeks.

David Leeke had recently left Shrewsbury Abbey, and was therefore available to stand in at short notice. He never really intended to return to S. Chad's where he had grown up and where he had received his musical training. He had, in fact, been offered the post by the then Vicar, Michael Pollit, on the departure of Roger Allen in 1983, but had felt it would be a mistake to return, and now he was faced with the same dilemma again, although this time he had been away from S. Chad's for a significantly longer period of time!

After the long incumbency of Bill Smallman (during which time he had fought valiantly against many odds to maintain the cathedral-like musical tradition) and the short spell of Sue Heath-Downey (who had swept aside any remnants of this with her passion that 'music is for all' and her desire to create something new and '21st century') there were many challenges for the new Director of Music. Even in her very short stay in post, Sue Heath-Downey had developed a new style of 'community music-making' and had set about building bridges between amateurs and professionals, something for which she has been well-known throughout her career. There were members of the congregation who embraced this new approach whilst others longed for the halcyon days of robed choirs and cathedral music to return.

David grasped the challenges to be faced with relish and sensitivity, and the musical fortunes of S. Chad's were well and truly revived under his direction, with choral services returned and the repertoire greatly expanded. David founded a choir of adults to sing the majority of the services, but a children's choir was also formed as well as a separate girls' choir. Kathryn Burningham (also Director of Music at University College, Oxford, and Director of Chapel Music at Shrewsbury School, 2008-2011) was appointed Director of Young People's Choirs and Coordinator of Musical Outreach. Kathryn was once herself an undergraduate music student at Merton College, Oxford, where she was organ scholar, and from where she graduated with a double-first degree. The introduction of a girls' choir at S. Chad's resulted in Choral Evensong being sung during the week in term time.

David was also fortunate enough to secure the services of Richard Walker who had moved to Shropshire after a very distinguished career in education. After reading music at Cambridge, Richard had been Assistant Organist of S. Mary's Cathedral, Edinburgh, before embarking on a life of teaching, firstly in Edinburgh in the 1970s when he was also Organist of S. John's, Princes Street, and from 1980-1985 he was Director of Music at the Leys School, Cambridge. He then spent twenty years as Director of Music at Harrow School. Richard was appointed Assistant Director of Music at S. Chad's in 2007 and, as well as playing for most of the major choral services, arranges the very successful 'Concerts in the Round' series. Concerts take place on most Friday lunchtimes of the year and have become an important part of the musical life of the town and the mission of S. Chad's as the town church. Audiences are buoyant and average around 90 to 100 people each week. One week per month is an organ recital, but other weeks can be as varied as jazz to mediaeval chamber music. Chetham's School of Music in Manchester and the Birmingham Conservatoire have both designated S. Chad's as one of their external performing venues and each undertake to provide one concert per term.

Another of David's innovations was to inaugurate an annual 'Shropshire Three Choirs' Festival with the choirs of S. Chad's, S. Laurence's, Ludlow and S. Oswald, Oswestry. These three churches are amongst a few in Shropshire which still have thriving SATB choirs in which children sing and play a part. This Festival rotates annually between each church with the resident Director of Music being the principal conductor and organiser every three years. The Festival was first held in Oswestry in 2009 under the direction of Michael Donkin, in S. Chad's in 2010 and in Ludlow in 2011 when Shaun Ward directed the choirs.

An annual Festival of Music has been held in recent years over the first bank holiday weekend in May and this has now become a firm part of the musical calendar not only of the church, but of the town and further afield. It has been set up as a separate charity with a board of trustees and a management committee. The constitution states that The Director of Music of S. Chad's is the Artistic Director of this festival. For the last three years this has concluded with the Festival Chorus singing a major work under the conductorship of David Leeke and accompanied by the English Symphony Orchestra. The Festival in 2009 ran from Friday 1 – Monday 4 May. A varied programme was offered: on Friday 1 May, Roy Woodhams (Vicar of Fleet, Hampshire) gave an organ recital. He also preached at the Festival Eucharist on Sunday 3 May. Also on that day there was a concert by Shrewsbury School String Ensemble, directed by the school's Head of Strings, David Joyce who has also been a good friend to S. Chad's over the years, and whose daughter Sally subsequently became a member of the girls' choir. On Saturday 2 May Christopher Symons gave a lecture and publicised his recent book on Sir Henry Walford Davies who had been born in Shropshire; Lauren Hibberd gave a piano recital and, in partnership with the Shropshire Music Trust, 'Black Voices' gave a concert. Lauren Hibberd had grown up in Shrewsbury and David Leeke was an encourager of her performances as a teenager. She subsequently studied at Chetham's School of Music and the Royal Northern College of Music in Manchester gaining a Masters' degree in piano accompaniment. On Sunday 3 May Trio Preti gave an excellent concert and Richard Walker gave an organ recital after Choral Evensong that day. On Monday 4 May the Hafren Wind Quintet played a concert and the Festival ended with Darwin Voices singing the 'Mass for Four Voices' by Williams Byrd and the 'Armed Man – A Mass for Peace' by Karl Jenkins.

In 2007 Mark Thomas was appointed the first Incumbent of the newly created United Benefice of Shrewsbury which includes S. Alkmund's (his predecessors had been Priest-in-Charge there from the middle 1980s). S. Alkmund's has undergone significant renovation since 2004, led largely by The Reverend Richard Hayes (appointed as Resident Priest there). Signal in this was the acquisition of the famous Harrison and Harrison organ of 1931 designed by Sydney Nicholson for the new School of English Church Music (later the Royal School of Church Music) at Chislehurst. This gem of an instrument has had several homes, but will be remembered by generations of students from its years in the chapel of Addington Palace. It came to S. Alkmund's in 2006 and was an integral part of the newly established 'Sam Baker School of Church Music', named after a much-loved former director of music at S. Chad's. Unfortunately this venture was not as successful as was hoped, and so was reconstituted and moved to S. Chad's in 2011. It is now known as 'The Sam Baker Trust' which has aims as follows:

- To support with educational programmes the liturgical and musical life of S. Chad's and other churches in Shrewsbury, Shropshire and the Marches. In doing so partnerships will be forged with other interested groups such as the RSCM, the Guild of Church Musicians, etc.
- To embrace, at the discretion of the Trustees, a wider appreciation of music in general and support for the music programme at S. Chad's. This is to include the promotion of an annual series of celebrity organ recitals, one of which is a Sam Baker Memorial Recital, as arranged by the Trust Director.

The Director of the Trust is David Leeke in his role as Director of Music at S. Chad's. Patrons of the Trust are Dr John Birch, Martin How, Dr Simon Preston and Dame Gillian Weir. The Trustees are: Julian and Richard Baker (Sam Baker's sons), Catherine Ennis (Chairman), Richard Lloyd and the Director of the RSCM, with The Reverend Prebendary David Crowhurst acting as Clerk to the Trustees and Administrator. A number of successful events have been held.

By 2008 S. Chad's organ was once again giving cause for concern. It had been in the care of Harrison and Harrison since the early 1980 and it was to them that the church turned for advice and an estimate for work to be undertaken. In August 2008 the then managing director of Harrison and Harrison, Mark Venning sent the following report:

I examined the organ on 13 June 2008. It has been in our care since we cleaned it and releathered the wind system in 1984; we have records of its maintenance history throughout that period, during which our tuner Duncan Bennett has looked after it and got to know it well. I have naturally consulted him in drawing up this report.

History
The organ was built by Norman & Beard in 1904. The design and construction are characteristically robust, and the same can be said of the organ's generously romantic sound.

In 1963 the organ was cleaned by Nicholson & Co., who provided a new console and converted the actions to electro-pneumatic operation. By 1982, when we first examined the organ, the leatherwork of the reservoirs and concussion bellows had reached the end of its life and was starting to leak. We therefore releathered the entire wind system in 1984, and cleaned the organ at the same time. In 2000 we renewed the drawstop solenoids at the console.

The organ retains its original specification, with the following exceptions:

- Nicholson added a 4ft Gemshorn to the Choir Organ in 1963; this was changed by us to a Tierce in 1990, when the Great Mixture was also revised. Nicholson also provided a Nazard $2^2/_3$ ft on the Choir, in place of an existing stop.
- In 1984 we extended the Pedal Violone to 8ft and 4ft pitch; the original 8ft extension of the Open Wood was removed.

The present situation

The organ has given good service since 1984, but in recent years signs of age have become apparent.
- The 1963 electrical system (for the couplers and pistons) has reached the end of its life.
- The Great, Swell and Choir soundboards have given a century of service without major overhaul. In addition to the effects of age, they have suffered some damage through overheating, and localised water damage. There are now some quite serious runnings.
- We are starting to experience troubles with the action leatherwork, both of the drawstop slider machines and of the key actions; these were last releathered in 1963.
- The pipework is once again becoming dirty, though this is not yet a serious issue.

The time has arrived for the church to start planning for major work on the organ. Ideally this would all be carried out as a single operation, but I have suggested a way in which it could be sub-divided, with work on the electrical system being undertaken first.

Console

This dates from 1963: it is well designed and its appearance is still good. In conjunction with the replacement of the coupler and switching systems, it is important that the electrical components should be brought up to date. We would overhaul the manual and pedal keyboards, and fit new contacts together with new thumb and foot piston units, retaining the present layout and adding eight general pistons, a setter piston, and advance and reverse pistons for a stepper.

The electric drawstop jamb mechanism was renewed in 2000, and is in good working order. The jambs and other woodwork would be cleaned and refurbished.

Electrical system

The coupler and piston systems are the same age as the console, and faults are now starting to appear. We would install new electronic coupler and piston systems; for the latter, we have allowed for 8 divisional and 64 general memories (more general memories are readily available if required).

Along with this work, new low-voltage cables, appropriately fused, would be installed throughout the organ; and new rectifiers would be provided, in order to ensure a compatible supply of low-voltage current for the new electronic systems. These would include dedicated rectifiers for the drawstop solenoids, which would allow the current to be suitably regulated for quiet operation.

Drawstop slider machines

There are clear signs that the leatherwork on these is failing. The machines would be fully overhauled and fitted with new magnets. If the work on the console and electrical system is carried out as a separate operation, it would be appropriate to do this work on the slider machines at the same time.

Key actions

For several years now we have had to deal with failing leather on the power motors, which date from 1963. Full overhaul and releathering would be undertaken, and new magnets would be fitted.

The pneumatic parts of these actions – the power motors – go back to the dependable Norman & Beard design, and deserve to be retained. (In this context, direct-electric actions would not perform so well). However the primary portion of the actions, dating from 1963, would benefit from improvement, and we would take the opportunity to re-design the actions with internal secondary valves, offering improved response. We would also design a similar electro-pneumatic action for the Swell high-pressure chest, which at present operates pneumatically from the main Swell electro-pneumatic action and, therefore, slightly behind it.

Soundboards and chests

It is evident that the slider soundboards have never undergone a major overhaul since they were first installed in 1904. With the passing of the years they have been affected by varying atmospheric conditions and, more recently, by some degree of overheating and by limited water damage to the Swell. Bad runnings are now apparent, especially on the Swell and Great. These soundboards are, however, excellently constructed and will respond well to a thorough overhaul and re-palleting. We have allowed for this in full: if less work proves to be needed once they are dismantled, a saving can be made.

The unit chests for the Pedal Organ would be releathered and fitted with new magnets. The pneumatic off-note machines would also be releathered (except for those of the Swell, which were releathered in 2002).

The electric chests for the Choir Tierce and Pedal top notes date from 1963 and are still in good working order.

Pipework

This is in good condition, though now becoming rather dirty. All would be thoroughly cleaned, metal flue pipes 4ft and less being washed to remove dirt from languids and flues; the longest 16ft basses would be cleaned in position. Stoppers would be re-fitted (the cork stoppers were replaced in 1984 and are in good condition.)

The reed pipes would be cleaned, wedges replaced where necessary, and loads re-fixed.

At the end of the work, all of the pipework would be carefully regulated by our voicer in order to reinstate the correct speech and balance; and the organ would be tuned through.

Wind system

This is in good condition, the reservoirs having been releathered in 1984. All of these would be cleaned out, and the system checked for leaks.

The concussion bellows were also releathered in 1984 and remain in good condition. We would re-site the Great concussion bellows, which would assist stability in this department and would help to prevent the Choir tremulant from disturbing the Great wind, which it does at present.

The two tremulants would be overhauled and releathered, as would the ventils for the unit chests.

Blower and humidifier

The blower is an excellent machine, and the humidifier is quite new. Both require, and receive, regular maintenance.

There are some sheets of insulation material lying near the blower. This material is flaking badly. Its purpose is not obvious, but it may originally have been intended to deaden the sound. I could not identify its nature, but I do not believe it to be harmful: however, I recommend that it should be removed in order to prevent fragments from being drawn into the organ's wind system.

General

The whole organ would be cleaned; the Swell and Choir shutters and their mechanism would be overhauled to take up wear. All parts of the mechanism would be checked and regulated, so as to leave everything in good working order.

Estimate

The above work could be carried out in two stages:
- A. The work under the headings of Console, Electrical system, and Drawstop slider machines could be carried out at a cost of £55,725.
- B. The remainder of the work could be carried out at a cost of £132,000.

There would be a saving of about £12,000 if the entire work were carried out as a single operation.

Possible additions

We do not propose any alterations to the present pipework: the organ's musical pedigree of 1904 can be clearly heard, and it gives a good account of itself. We discussed the possibility of making certain stops playable on different departments (Great Tromba on Choir and Pedal; Swell Bourdon and Fagotto on Pedal), but I feel that I must advise against this, as the additional mechanism would cause overcrowding and maintenance difficulties.

Two additions might, however, be possible:

1. *It has been suggested that a Tuba stop could be added alongside the Choir swell-box, in the space over the passage way. This is not an obvious place for such a stop, well to the back of the organ and speaking sideways; but the unusual architecture of the church is in our favour, and I believe that the transmission of sound along the curved outer wall of the church could be both effective and exciting.*

In order to make a Tuba in the appropriate style for this organ, we would need to provide it with its own independent wind system – i.e. blower and reservoir – as well as a new chest and electro-pneumatic action. It amounts to a considerable amount of work and – subject to final design – we estimate that the cost would be in the region of £30,000.

2. *It would be possible to add an 8ft Posaune on the Pedal Organ, as an extension of the 16ft Trombone. A chest and 12 pipes would be required, together with an extra drawstop at the console. The cost would be £6,900.*

The following items are excluded:

- VAT. (The great majority of the work, apart from additions or enhancements, would qualify for refund of VAT under the Listed Places of Worship Grant Scheme).
- Mains electrical work (connection of the new rectifiers and Tuba blower; any improvements in the lighting within the organ and at the console. All the mains wiring should be checked).
- Provision of scaffolding and lifting gear for Stage B; provision of working facilities.
- Transport, charged at cost.
- Any work on the blower and humidifier (none is expected).
- Any increase in costs after 31 December 2008.

———————————

Such extensive work is required only very seldom in an organ's lifetime. This instrument is very well built, and thorough restoration will give excellent, long-lasting results. For the sake of comparison it is worth bearing in mind that the cost of building an organ of this size today would be in the region of £507,000 excluding VAT, and this is the sum for which the present instrument should be insured.

I will gladly answer any questions on this report, or return to Shrewsbury for further discussions if that will be helpful.

M B Venning
Director
6 August 2008

The PCC embraced this report with enthusiasm and Harrison and Harrison were asked to undertake the work, which they could not fit into their schedule until 2011, giving sufficient time to begin the necessary steps to raise the funds required.

Further discussions took place between David Leeke and Harrison and Harrison which amended the original quote in some ways. The organ was taken out for restoration in January 2011 and returned by October 2011, during which time the church managed with a two manual Allen electronic organ to accompany the services, and there were no recitals. A letter sent to David Leeke dated 21 February 2011 is appended below giving an update on a number of requests which David Leeke and Richard Walker had made to the firm.

We very much look forward to the work at S. Chad's.

At our visit, we discussed options that are under consideration, as described in our email of 14 October 2010. The costs are detailed below at 2011 rates:

- *The main work, which is included in the agreement of December 2009 will cost £191,041 plus VAT*
  The following options are not included in our agreement and the additional costs would be:
- *To install a Tuba will be £32,371.*
- *To install a **Great to Choir** coupler will cost £691.*
- *To install a **Unison-off** coupler on the Choir will cost £691.*
- *To install the Swell Viol d'Orchestre on the Choir in place of the Dulciana 8ft, and install a Fifteenth 2ft on the vacated slide in the Swell will cost £4774. We have confirmed that the Dulciana is a full-compass stop.*
- *To re-order the composition of the Swell Mixture will cost £2321.*
- *To increase the number of general piston memories to 128, rather than providing 64 as included in our agreement, will cost £150.*

The above prices do not include VAT which will be applied at the standard rate. It is assumed they would be carried out at the same time as the main work. I would be grateful if you could confirm as soon as possible whether they are to go ahead.

Please get in touch if you have any questions.

Yours sincerely
Nancy Radford
Administrator

More correspondence followed as the copy of an email of 20 March 2011 which David Leeke sent to Durham indicates:

Dear Duncan/Nancy

Please take this as authority to proceed with the following additions/alterations to the organ at S. Chad's, Shrewsbury.

Please include in your work (and charged as per your latest email of 9 March 2011):
Tuba stop £32, 371

Transfer the Viol d'Orchestre from the swell to the choir (in place of the Dulciana) and install a Fifteenth (or similar stop - ie not a piccolo) on the swell in the vacated slide. Cost £4,774 [As I mentioned on the phone we may be able to finance this in memory of my late Mother]

Reorder the composition of the Swell Mixture. Cost £2321
Install a Choir Unison Off. Cost £691

If the Tuba works on the Octave and Sub Octave couplers as already requested, and the Great Tromba can also be playable from the Choir (see below), we will probably not require a Great to Choir coupler. We do not wish to proceed with the additional memory on the general pistons.

In talking to your staff when they were on site, we understand that they suggested that it was possible to make certain other desirable amendments which Mark Venning had suggested were impossible. These include having the heavy pressure Swell reeds playable on the pedal, and having the Great Tromba playable on both the pedal and the choir organs. Having a softer 16' pedal reed for playing such things as Bach Preludes and Fugues would be really useful, and a 4' pedal reed would be good for some of the Bach Choral Preludes etc.

I can see how this might be done with the swell reeds, as they are on their own soundboard and chest, but am at a loss to know/see if this is possible with the Great Tromba which is on the same soundboard/chest as the rest of the Great organ. Perhaps you could advise if any of this is possible, and, if so, what the cost would be? We will confirm our thoughts/comments by return.

All good wishes

David
David Leeke
Organist & Director of Music,
S. Chad's, Shrewsbury

The new Flageolet on the swell organ was funded in memory of Connie Leeke (David's mother) who died during the organ renovations. Connie's funeral raised much of the necessary money together with a substantial gift she had made at the start of the restoration project. She had been a faithful worshipper at S. Chad's for most of her long life. She was a great supporter of all the church's musical pursuits and a huge encourager of her son, and so this was a fitting memorial to her.

The Great to Choir stop was added. The Tromba was not made playable on either the choir or pedal organs as it would require its own soundboard for this to be possible and the organ layout is very cramped and does not allow the space for this. The swell reeds were also not made playable elsewhere for reasons set out by Mark Venning in 2008.

On 1 April 2011 Duncan Mathews (the works manager at Harrison and Harrison sent the following note to David Leeke (copying in Duncan Bennett, the organ's regular tuner):

Dear David

The Organ
I enclose drawings of the console layout for your comment.

Jambs
The jamb layout has been revised to include the additional stops: the dotted lines represent the position of items that have been moved. We have relocated the Choir and Swell couplers to the bottom of their respective plates and have raised the Great to Pedal pistons combination coupler to create space for the piston control panel.

You will note that, for the present, the Swell Viol d'Orchestre knob retains its original name following its move to the Choir, though I recollect that you had it in mind to tune one of the Choir strings as a Céleste; please let me know if you would like this to be re-engraved.

Piston layout
The piston layout is as we discussed. The stepper foot pistons will be set on raised pattressses.

Piston control panel
There are two possible piston control panel layouts. The first, with three digits, is for use with 64 general memory levels, the second shows the additional digit required for 128 memory levels; both are prepared for future enlargement of the system. The second panel includes scrolling in tens, which is useful when the number of memory levels is more than 100.

I would be grateful for your comments on these as soon as possible.

Our contract includes the provision of 64 general memory levels, as previously advised the additional cost of 128 memory levels will be £150 plus VAT; please let me know whether you would like us to provide the additional memory.

Yours sincerely
D P Mathews
Works Manager

David Leeke replied enthusiastically to this, agreeing that the old swell Viol d'Orchestre should be renamed Violoncello Celeste and that 64 general memory levels would be adequate for future use. The company worked on the instrument in situ from early July to its completion and all agreed that, under the leadership of Jaroslav Strazovsky, they were a credit to themselves and the company. The church still suffers from varying temperatures, though not to the extent of those complained about by Reg Harwood in the 1960s. Heat rises and the swell organ is right against the roof of the nave; this hampers stable tuning. The Discus humidifier helps here, but the organ does still suffer from the fluctuating temperatures which are a feature of S. Chad's. On sunny days the sun pours in through the large windows on the Quarry side of the church and these rays are frequently pointing straight at the organ.

From March to May 2010 Richard Walker gave 16 very well-received recitals playing the complete organ works of J. S. Bach to help draw attention to the organ appeal. Good audiences enjoyed this marathon series, and Richard raised a significant sum towards the cost of the organ's restoration. It is hoped that this series will be repeated on the restored organ in 2014.

Coinciding with David's appointment to S. Chad's, he assumed the conductorship of Shrewsbury Cantata Choir. Under his leadership, this local choral society have held most of their concerts in S. Chad's, some accompanied with orchestra as the chosen works required, but several accompanied on the organ. Timothy Noon (a friend of David's from when they were both in Kent) often accompanied these superbly until he became no longer available as he took up the post of Director of Music at Auckland Cathedral in New Zealand in September 2011!

There have been a number of broadcasts on national and local radio since David came to S. Chad's, and signal in that were three BBC TV 'Songs of Praise' programmes filmed in the autumn of 2008. One was broadcast for Remembrance Sunday that year and another for Christmas. The third programme went out in 2009 and commemorated Shrewsbury's most famous son, Charles Darwin who was baptised in S. Chad's. The church choir had an important role in each of these programmes and the church hosted 900 people for each of the recordings. Included in this assembled group was Shrewsbury Cantata Choir and members of the local armed forces. Pupils from local schools including Shrewsbury School and Shrewsbury High School were directed by Kathryn Burningham. S. Chad's Girls' Choir, under her direction also appeared on BBC Radio 4 in Holy Week 2012.

In November 2008 Shrewsbury Cantata Choir gave a concert, accompanied by Timothy Noon which included Parry's 'I was glad', Vaughan Williams' 'Five Mystical Songs' and Britten's 'Rejoice in the Lamb' as well as music by Howells and Finzi. Richard Walker played Messiaen's 'La Nativité du Seigneur' on the centenary of the birth of Messiaen (10 December 2008) which was accompanied by slides of Our Lord's nativity. The moving combination of music and art was especially enthusiastically received.

To celebrate the 200th anniversary of the birth of Mendelssohn, David Leeke conducted the Cantata Choir and orchestra in Mendelssohn's 'Elijah' in March 2009, and the Cantata Choir sang a programme of choral classics with Timothy Noon (organ) in the summer of 2009. S. Chad's Chamber Choir, Darwin Voices, which was formed around this time, gave a concert of passiontide music in 2010 which included the little-performed 'Stabat Mater' by d'Astorga. The upper voices of the church choir sang Pergolesi's 'Stabat Mater' on Palm Sunday 2010. Also in March 2010, the Cantata Choir sang various psalm settings, again accompanied by Timothy Noon. These included Bruckner's 'Psalm 150', Bernstein's 'Chichester Psalms', Monteverdi's 'Beatus vir' and Patterson's 'Canterbury Psalms'. On 27 March, 2010, S. Chad's girls' choir sang the ripieno part in Bach's S. Matthew Passion which was performed by the Phoenix Singers. Timothy Noon returned to play for the Cantata Choir's summer concert in 2010 in which David Leeke arranged music for Royal occasions including Handel's 'Coronation Anthems' and Walton's 'Coronation Te Deum'. Darwin Voices sang a concert of European sacred music in October 2010 and a concert of Christmas music entitled 'O magnum mysterium', including several settings of that text.

Shrewsbury Cantata Choir performed Bach's 'S. Matthew Passion' in March 2011 collaborating successfully with Moreton Hall School Choir, and in April 2011 Darwin Voices gave a concert of music associated with Our Lord's death and resurrection. The Festival in 2011 began with another TV broadcast – this time live. On Friday 29 April, Darwin Voices sang music for Royal Occasions to commemorate the wedding that day in Westminster Abbey of HRH Prince William and Catherine Middleton. Graham Walker, international cellist and son of Richard and Gay Walker, gave a master class with local students who also performed at the lunchtime concert on Saturday 30 April, and Graham gave a concert that evening. The day's activities ended with folk music presented by The Boscastle Busker fresh from his recent appearances on BBC TV. Sunday 1 May 2011 seemed to be yet another day commemorating S. Chad's links with Sam Baker and his family. At lunchtime Katherine Baker (Sam's granddaughter), Principal Flute in the Hallé Orchestra gave a flute recital accompanied by her brother Jonathan. After Choral Evensong that night, Sam's son, Julian, father of the above duo, gave an illustrated talk entitled 'My Life in Music'. The Festival concluded with the Festival Chorus and the ESO giving a performance of Handel's 'Messiah'.

The Cantata Choir also performed Brahms' 'Requiem' and Vaughan Williams' 'Hodie' in the autumn of 2011, the latter being skilfully accompanied on the restored organ by Richard Walker.

From 2007, S. Chad's choirs became increasingly active; visits have been made to sing services at Portsmouth, Birmingham, Salisbury and Wakefield Cathedrals as well as a number of churches. They gave a concert of English Church music at S. Mary's Gomersall where Mark Thomas was vicar in the 1980s. An annual concert given by the children takes place jointly with the children from S. Oswald's, Oswestry (alternating venues) in July each year. Links are being forged with local schools and the

County Music Service and the church is in ever greater demand as a venue for concerts. Since David came to S. Chad's the church has benefited from a number of commissions. Compositions have been received from composers including Richard Lloyd, Simon Lole, Timothy Noon, Christopher Mabley, Adrian Williams and Martin How. Some of these have been commissioned for the annual Festival and others to mark specific occasions, such as 'S. Chad's Mass' by Adrian Williams, written in memory of David's mother. Adrian Williams and David were fellow students at the Royal College of Music in the 1970s.

David's liturgical expertise was marked by the church as part of wider staff restructuring in 2011/12. In 2012, David was promoted to 'Director of Music and Liturgy' to head up a team forming a music and liturgy department.

Also in early 2012, the organ was reopened after its extensive restoration and rebuild with a series of celebrity recitals. The inaugural recital was given by Dr Roy Massey, MBE, well-known in the area having been at Hereford Cathedral for many years before his retirement and a former President of both the RCO and the Cathedral Organists' Association. It was fitting that this recital was given by Roy, a friend to the church for many years, and maintaining the link with Hereford, as one of Roy's predecessors at Hereford, Dr Melville Cook, gave the inaugural recital after the Nicholson rebuild in 1963. The second recital was presented by Simon Preston, who had come pretty much each year with a choir in the days of Sam Baker's incumbency, and, as part of the resident team of musicians, Richard Walker gave a splendid recital on a most filthy night in February 2012. Recitals through 2012 feature all but one of the previous Directors of Music still living, and in the same year the John Stainer Scholarship Fund was founded for the provision of future organ (and also other music) scholars.

S. Chad's Choir c.1935
Choirmaster: Austin Herbert

S. Chad's Choir c.1964

S. Chad's Choir c.1972

S. Chad's Choir, July 1973 at Portsmouth Cathedral with Rev. Robert Willis, Curate, and Sam Baker, Choirmaster (back row, 7 from left)

Right: S. Chad's Choir, 1981 at Liverpool Cathedral. In the photograph is Rev Philip Chester, Curate, David Grundy, Choirmaster, (back row, 3 from left)and Ernest Pratt, Assistant Organist of Liverpool Cathedral

Bottom right: S. Chad's Choir, 1982, Roger Allen, Choirmaster (extreme left)

Bottom left: S. Chad's Adult Choir, April 2012. David Leeke, Choirmaster (bottom left), Richard Walker, Assistant Director of Music (bottom right), Kathryn Burningham (5 from top) and Prebendary Mark Thomas (Vicar)

Above: *S. Chad's organ console 1904*

Top right: *S. Chad's organ pipes*

Right: *S. Chad's organ console*

Right: *S. Chad's organ stops, left and right-hand sides*

From top left:

Austin Herbert

Reg Harwood

Sam Baker

David Grundy

Roger Allen

Bill Smallman

Sue Heath-Downey

David Leeke

Part 2 –
THE MUSICIANS

Organists of S. Chad's

EDMUND BAKER (d.1765)
(S. Chad's before 1716 – 1727)

It seems that Edmund Baker was simultaneously organist of both S. Chad's and S. Mary's! At that time, both churches were under the jurisdiction of the Mayor and Corporation, and a document *"sealed and delivered these words"* by the Mayor records his name in both places. Edmund had been a pupil of the organist and composer, John Blow.

A document in the Shropshire Archives written in 1846 recalls that Mr Baker was succeeded *"on his death"* by Mr James Burney. This is in fact the same Edmund Baker who became Organist at Chester Cathedral in 1727 succeeding Benjamin Worrall.

Edmund seems quite a rebellious character, as he was once *"admonished by the Dean and Chapter for refusing to sing in an Anthem at Evening Service when requested to do so by the Senior Prebendary"*. However, so many stories abound about the bad behaviour of the choirmen and bedesmen (and also a previous unknown organist who was dismissed twice!) that perhaps Edmund's transgression was not really that noteworthy!

When in post at Chester Cathedral, he was almost incapacitated by gout and, having no regular deputy, was probably quite relieved when his pupil Charles Burney (younger half-brother of James Burney who was organist at S. Chad's, q.v. – more likely at S. Mary's) managed to learn enough chants to *"keep the organ going"*.

In the spring of 1742, Edmund Baker met Handel who was on his way to Dublin to organise the first performance of 'Messiah'. The 'Messiah' part-books had been hastily transcribed, and when Handel was delayed in Chester for several days waiting for the wind to change before embarking, some of the cathedral singers were involved in singing through the choruses to check their accuracy. The organ in the Cathedral at that time (and therefore later reputed to have been played by Handel even though most reports of the incident state that the rehearsals took place in the 'Golden Falcon' inn in

Northgate Street, where Handel was lodging) was subsequently moved to St. Paul's Pro-Cathedral in Valletta, Malta.

Edmund died in 1765 and was buried in the South Choir Aisle of Chester Cathedral on 5 February 1765. His successor as Cathedral Organist was Edward Orme.

JAMES BURNEY (c1709 – 17 June 1789)
(S. Chad's 1732 – 1784)

Unfortunately, there is no record of who succeeded Edmund Baker at S. Chad's on his departure to Chester in 1727, and there seems to be a gap until 1732; we know that James Burney was *"organist at St Mary's Church, Shrewsbury from 1732-1786"* and, as the two town churches were then both under the jurisdiction of the Corporation, it would not be an unfair assumption that he was also at S. Chad's from the same time.

James was a son of James Macburney (born in Great Hanwood in 1678; died 1749) by his first wife. Macburney, who was a dancer, violinist and painter, changed the family name to Burney around 1726, about the time of the birth of his youngest children (twins Charles and Susanna) by his second wife.

James had been *"Organist of both St. Mary's and St. Chad's"* for about a decade when, in the early 1740s, he gave lessons for three years to his young half-brother, Charles (who was later to become the eminent musicologist). Charles had returned to Shrewsbury after leaving the public school at Chester aged 15 or 16 where his music master had been the Cathedral Organist, Edmund Baker (who had himself previously been organist of S. Chad's - q.v.).

James continued to be organist of both churches for the next 40-odd years, and we know that his immediate successor at S. Chad's was John Wynne (who became Organist in 1784). James's death on 17 June 1789 (in the *"80th year of his age"*) occurred *"three years after leaving S. Mary's"*, so it is possible that he might have played for a little while solely at S. Mary's to help out John who was very young on his appointment to the post at S. Chad's.

James was buried in S. Mary's on 19 June 1789; a memorial tablet *"with appropriate musical emblems"* stating that James had been organist of the church for 54 years was placed in the nave of S. Mary's; this still existed in 1893, but sadly it was no longer there by 1920, and there is no record of when or why it was removed from the church.

JOHN WYNNE (1772 – 1 January 1860)
(S. Chad's 1784 – 1846)

There is a record of a baptism of a John Wynne (*"son of John and Sarah"*) in S. Chad's Church on 31 January 1772, and this date tallies with the deduced year of birth from the 1851 census when John stated he was 79.

John became Organist at S. Chad's in 1784 when he was only 12, and had therefore only been Organist for less than four years when the church fell down in 1788.

It seems likely that John Wynne married Ann Griffiths on 23 December 1798, and by 1841 John was living in Swan Hill, but there is no apparent record of Ann in the household, just a Mary and a Jane who may have been John's sisters.

The 1851 census confirmed that John was a widower and was then living in College Hill. He was described as a *"Gentleman and Landed Proprietor"*, and blind; his three sisters, Elizabeth, Jane and Catherine, were living with him.

John Wynne died on 1 January 1860 of *"old age"*; his occupation being listed as *"proprietor of houses"*, and an obituary to him appeared in the local paper later that month.

WALTER CECIL HAY (7 August 1828 – 1 October 1905)
(before 1865 – after 1881)

Walter Cecil Hay was born in Shrewsbury on 7 August, 1828, the oldest of five children born to watch-maker Thomas William Hay and his wife Cecilia (born in Holloway, Middlesex). He was baptised in Swan Hill Independent Chapel on 18 August 1829. It is almost certain that Walter, after living with his family in Market Square later studied at the Royal Academy of Music in London before he married Emily Henshaw from Oswestry in the spring of 1855. As conductor of the Whitchurch Choral Society, he taught the young Edward German (born in that town) who was a talented musician. Walter managed to persuade German's parents that their son should try for a place at the Royal Academy of Music and German duly enrolled there in 1880 to study organ and violin, later becoming a well-respected composer.

The census for 1871 shows that Walter - occupation *"Artist (Music)"* and his wife Emily – occupation *"Artist (Painting)"* were living in Market Square, Shrewsbury, with their son Walter (aged 15) and daughter Amy (13); their next door neighbour was a pianoforte maker and tuner. By the following census (in 1881), the Hays (with Amy, and their 9 year old daughter Nina) were living at Dogpole Court describing themselves as *"Professor of Music"* and *"Wife of Professor"*.

There is no record of Walter's resignation from S. Chad's, but this had occurred by 1884. The census shows that the Hays did not leave the area as in 1891 they were living at 2 Claremont Bank.

Kelly's Directory of Shropshire for 1900 as well the census of the following year show that W C Hay's address was still 2 Claremont Bank, and it seems that the family remained there until Walter died, aged 77, in 1905.

BENJAMIN PRITCHARD (20 April 1860 – 23 May 1927)
(S. Chad's 1884 – before 1911)

Benjamin Pritchard was born in Shrewsbury on 20 April 1860, the son of William (who was from Astley Abbots) and Lucy (nee Hewitt) from Madeley. He was the 4th child of 7, and unlike most of his siblings he did not enter his father's nursery and seeds business. The family home was at Nursery Cottages, New Street in the census of 1871 and 1881, and by the latter census Benjamin could describe himself as *"Professor of Music"*.

Benjamin married Margaret Ann Bulmer from Leeds in 1882, and, by the time of his appointment as Organist of St. Chad's, the couple had a baby son, Reginald, who, according to the 1911 census, grew up to become a *"Church Organ Tuner"*.

Benjamin Pritchard became Organist of S. Chad's on 2 November 1884, and the census of 1891 shows Benjamin and Margaret with their five children (Reggie, Dorothy, Robert, Elsie and Leslie) and two servants living at 49 Belle Vue Road.

Kelly's Directory of Shropshire for 1900 gives 16 Berwick Street as the address for the Pritchards, and the 1901 census shows that Benjamin had become an insurance inspector to supplement his income as Organist, and the family plus three servants were now living at Fairfield, Berwick Road. It is difficult to pinpoint exactly when he relinquished his duties as Organist at S. Chad's, the latest possibility being 1910. By 1911, the Pritchards were living at Sefton House, The Mount, but they later moved to Port Hill. Benjamin died in Berrington Hospital in Condover on 23 May 1927.

WALTER BROWNING EBRALL, (1860 – 12 August 1936)
(S. Chad's before 1911 – 1933)

Walter Browning Ebrall was born in Shrewsbury in late 1860, the youngest son of a banker's clerk, Samuel Browning Ebrall and Alice (née Parkes) who came from Oakengates. The Ebralls and their two youngest children (Lucy and Walter) plus two servants were living at 'Lucerne' in Oakley Street in the census of 1881.

The two older children (Frederick and Alice) were at home for the 1891 census – by this time the family were living in Meole Brace, the father having risen to the post of bank manager (of the Salop Old Bank in the Square), and Frederick (later better known as F W Ebrall, organ builder) now learning his trade as an engine maker's apprentice.

Walter started his musical career as an organ builder's clerk (probably in his brother's firm) according to the 1901 census, and by 1911 could describe himself as *"Professor of Music"*. By this time he had gained his ARCO and gave many organ recitals in the church as well as greatly expanding the choir's repertoire.

It seems that he was considered by all to have been a fine player, but, in fact, there appear to be very few records of Walter's actual musical achievements during his tenure as Organist (considerably over twenty years). This might be partly a result of the Great War and its aftermath, but, for whatever reason, in later years his name was sadly almost forgotten by those involved with the musical life of the town. His elder brother, Frederick William, the organ-builder and music dealer (who advertised regularly in the Musical Times) was much more well-known than him in the early part of the 20th century, but, 100 years on, the unusual surname is probably most connected with the local firm of Gunmakers and Ammunition Dealers which closed in the early years of the 21st century.

Walter Ebrall married Emily Bailey at Meole Brace in the summer of 1921. Although the couple continued to live in Shrewsbury (at 'Holmleigh', Belle Vue Gardens) after Walter's retirement from S. Chad's in 1933, he died (possibly while on holiday) in Dyffryn, Merionethshire on 12 August 1936. The administrators of his will were his widow, Emily, and his brother, Frederick William (described as a "motor engineer") and the probate records shows that he left quite substantial effects (£7,526 15s 5d).

FREDERICK AUSTIN HERBERT (13 May 1896 – 21 July 1989)
(S. Chad's 1933 – 1946)

Frederick Austin Herbert was born in Hereford, the eldest child of Evelyn Sarah (née Rowe), who had also been born in the city and her husband, Leicestershire-born Stephen Austin Herbert who was a solicitor's clerk. Austin was a traditional family name given to all the sons as a middle name, but Frederick chose to use it as the name by which he would be known. It seems that Austin was probably a chorister at Hereford Cathedral under George Robertson Sinclair (immortalised in Elgar's Enigma Variations with his bulldog, Dan). Austin's younger brother Alexander was certainly a cathedral chorister, and it is likely that Austin had his organ lessons from Sinclair at the cathedral. By 1911 it seems that, like his father, Austin was also a solicitor's clerk, but he was soon to study at the Birmingham and Midland School of Music (now the Birmingham Conservatoire).

At Birmingham Austin gained several qualifications, FRCO, LRAM and ARCM (the passing of his LRAM Piano Teaching Diploma being listed in The Musical Times of November 1921). He married Alice Maude Unitt (from Hoole, Chester) in the summer of 1918, having served in the Great War as a corporal in the Cheshire Regiment. Before his appointment to S. Chad's on the retirement of Ebrall in 1933, he had been Music Master at Saltley Secondary School, Birmingham. He also taught harmony and theory at the Birmingham School of Music, a post he continued to hold during his time at S. Chad's and beyond. Although Austin Herbert resigned from S. Chad's in 1946, he continued to live in Shrewsbury, dying here in July 1989 at the grand age of 93.

REGINALD GEORGE HARWOOD (10 May 1901 – 19 September 1971)
(S. Chad's 1946 – 1971)

Reg Harwood was born in Colchester, the eldest of the four sons of handicraft teacher Thomas (born in West Ham, London) and his wife Ada (née Lait).

Although the family appeared to have moved to Bath during Reg's childhood, his first organist's posts were in Colchester, at S. Nicholas' (aged 18), and subsequently at S. Stephen's. Reg studied with W F Kingdon (the Organist of S. Lawrence Jewry in the City of London) and Sir Walter Parratt (Organist of S. George's Chapel, Windsor) at the Royal College of Music, gaining the B.Mus (London) degree as well as his FRCO.

Reg became Organist of S. Luke's, Charlton and Music Master at Shirley House School before becoming Organist of S. Peter's, Petersfield and Music Master of Churcher's College from 1924-1944. Immediately before his appointment at S. Chad's in 1946, he was Organist of All Saints', Headingley and Music Master at Oxford Boys' School.

Reg moved to Shrewsbury with his wife, Alice <u>Barbara</u> (née Steward) whom he had married in 1924, and their teenage son, Ian (who was later to become a lute professor at the RCM), to take up his post at S. Chad's and to be Assistant Director of Music at Shrewsbury School. He succeeded the late Freddie Morris as Conductor of Shrewsbury Choral Society in 1951 and was also Conductor of Oswestry Choral Society. Reg was also President of the Shrewsbury and District Organists' and Choirmasters' Association on several occasions. He was always regarded as a true gentleman, and gave devoted service to S. Chad's for twenty five years, retiring from all his posts in June 1971. Although he retired to Cambridgeshire to be closer to his son Ian, who was a Lay Clerk in Ely Cathedral Choir, Reg sadly died just a few months later on 19 September.

ALFRED <u>SAMUEL</u> WENSLEY BAKER (28 May 1907 – 17 August 1980)
(S. Chad's 1971 – 1975)

Sam Baker was born in Prenton, Cheshire, the second child of London-born Alfred William Baker and Naomi Elizabeth Wensley who came from New Brighton, Cheshire. The family lived at 127 Temple Road and in the 1911 census Sam's father was listed as an *"Agent and Merchant – Wholesale Drapery"*. He and his boyhood friend, Caleb Jarvis (for many years City Organist of Liverpool) received their organ lessons at Liverpool Cathedral with Walter Henry Goss Custard. Sam was educated at Birkenhead School, before entering Lichfield Theological College. Ordination did not follow, but rather further musical study with George Oldroyd at S. Michael's, Croydon and at Trinity College of Music, London where he gained diplomas from Trinity College of Music and the Royal College of Organists.

In 1936 Sam was appointed Organist of Christleton Parish Church (Chester) and one of the assistant organists of Chester Cathedral (where he taught a chorister called George Guest, later to be in charge of the music at S. John's College, Cambridge for many years). Sam married Evelyn Perry Brown in

Cambridge in late 1937. They had two sons: Richard who was a Chorister at King's College, Cambridge under Boris Ord, returning there as an undergraduate choral scholar under Sir David Willcocks; and Julian, who was a chorister at Lichfield Cathedral under Ambrose Porter and who was a professional horn player, becoming Principal Horn in The Hallé Orchestra and subsequently the BBC Symphony Orchestra and the Orchestra of the Royal Opera House, Covent Garden as well as a Professor of Horn at the Royal College of Music.

In 1942 Sam and his young family moved to Ellesmere College, Shropshire, where Sam joined the music staff. In 1945 he became Assistant Organist of Derby Cathedral and a member of the music staff at Repton School and its Preparatory School, Foremarke Hall. Here he was to teach one of the school's music scholars, Martin J R How, known to so many through a lifetime's distinguished work with the RSCM.

Sam moved to Shrewsbury in 1951 to take up the post of Organist and Choirmaster at S. Mary's. For sixteen years, Sam directed one of the most distinguished parish choirs in the country at S. Mary's, and became a national figure in the field of choir training and organ extemporisation. During these years, he was also Director of Music at Adams' Grammar School, Newport. On the retirement of Reg Harwood in 1971, Sam moved to S. Chad's, and although he himself retired to west Wales in 1975, he was to make a huge impact on the musical life of this church.

Retirement was to be dogged by increasingly failing health and Sam died less than five years after leaving S. Chad's. He is buried in the church yard at S. Dogmaels near Cardigan. In more recent years, his name has been immortalised at S. Chad's through The Sam Baker Trust.

RICHARD DAVID STEPHENS (b. 4 September 1946)
(S. Chad's 1975 – 1977)

Richard Stephens grew up in Monmouthshire and had organ lessons at Llandaff Cathedral with Robert Joyce and at Hereford Cathedral with Melville Cook before studying at Trinity College of Music with Martin Neary and John Webster. He subsequently studied with Marie Clare Alain in Paris before embarking upon a career as a teacher. He was Organist of S. Augustine's, Kilburn in north London and Head of Music at S. Augustine's School before coming to Shrewsbury as Director of Music at the Priory Boys' Grammar School in 1974. Richard succeeded Sam Baker at S. Chad's in 1975, and during this time he was also conductor of the Concord Singers. Although Richard's time at S. Chad's was short, he maintained the musical life of the church and under his direction the choir toured extensively in the area.

Richard moved from Shrewsbury to assume the role of Director of Music at Moreton Hall Girls' School, Oswestry, where he remained for 15 years before holding a similar post at Mount S. Mary's College in Derbyshire. During this time he was also lecturer in choral music at Bretton Hall College and director of the college choir. Since 2001 Richard has been Director of Music at S. James' Chipping Campden where he is also much involved with the Chipping Campden Festival.

DAVID HEYWOOD GRUNDY (12 September, 1934 – 29 July, 2010)
(S. Chad's 1977 – 1981)

David Grundy was born in Accrington and educated at Thornes House Grammar School, Wakefield. He received his initial musical education with the Director of Music at Thornes House, Margaret Markland who instilled in him a love of choirs and choral music, and had piano lessons from Douglas Woolsey. He subsequently studied at the Royal Academy of Music – organ with Dr Arthur Pritchard, and Douglas Hawkridge, piano with Patrick Cory and composition with Dr Eric Thiman. Here he gained his London B Mus degree as well as the LRAM, ARCM and ARCO diplomas. During this time David became Assistant Organist of All Souls', Langham Place, W1, and Organist of S. Mary's Islington.

In 1961, David embarked upon his teaching career as a member of the music staff at S. Lawrence College, Ramsgate, and subsequently as Director of Music at Kingham Hill School, (a sister foundation to Oakhill Theological College) Oxfordshire in 1964. He moved to Shropshire to succeed Sam Baker as Director of Music at Adams' Grammar School, Newport in 1971, moving to Shrewsbury in 1974 to become Director of Music at the Wakeman School (then a Grammar School). When Shrewsbury's education system turned comprehensive, David became Director of Music at Shrewsbury Sixth Form College from 1981 until his retirement in 1996, and it was in his early days here that he obtained a Masters' degree in education. David was to live in Shrewsbury for over thirty years, and for all of that time had a close musical association with S. Chad's. He was conductor of Shrewsbury Choral Society from 1974 – 2001 and of Shrewsbury Symphony Orchestra from 1985 – 2005. His love of orchestral music was nurtured by his frequent attendance at The Yorkshire Symphony Orchestra rehearsals and concerts about which he wrote a book called 'The Glorious Experiment'.

Although David was only 'in charge' of the music at S. Chad's for four years (other pressures of work precluded a lengthier stint), he remained part of the church's musical team, serving off and on as Assistant Director of Music from 1981-2005.

In 2005, David and his wife Judy retired to Eastbourne and David became heavily involved in music in East Sussex, most especially at S. Saviour's, Eastbourne. In retirement, David and his colleague and friend, The Revd John Waddington Feather collaborated on words and music for several hymns and short cantatas based on biblical characters. Sadly, David died suddenly in 2010. His funeral was held at S. Saviour's, Eastbourne and this was later followed by a memorial service at S. Chad's.

ROGER WILLIAM ALLEN (b. 3 December, 1951)
(S. Chad's 1981 – 1984)

Roger Allen began his musical career as a chorister at the Church of S. Matthew, Northampton where he studied the organ under Michael Nicholas. He subsequently read Music at the University of Liverpool (1971-75) where he was also Organist of Mossley Hill Parish Church. He was actively involved in the music of Liverpool Anglican Cathedral, studying the organ with Noel Rawsthorne and working alongside the then Cathedral Choirmaster, Ronald Woan, and gained the degrees of BA and B Mus as well as an ARCM diploma.

From 1975-1981 Roger was Assistant Director of Music at Ellesmere College where he taught with Directors of Music Anthony Dowlen and Paul Spicer. He then enjoyed a brief but (to him!) memorable period as Organist of S. Chad's, during which time he also held teaching appointments at Shrewsbury School and Prestfelde Preparatory School. Under Roger, the choir of S. Chad's (then still men and boys) flourished with an input of boys from Prestfelde.

Roger subsequently moved to Oxford as Director of Music at New College Choir School where he worked closely with the College organist, Edward Higginbottom. This appointment enabled him to revive his research interests in late nineteenth- century music and complete his doctoral thesis on the German conductor and composer, Wilhelm Furtwängler, obtaining the degrees of MA (Oxon) and D Phil (Oxon). In 2001 he moved permanently into the University sector as Lecturer and Director of Studies in Music at S. Peter's College where he was later appointed Fellow and Tutor in Music (2006) and Dean (2007). Roger is also Director of Music at S. Peter's and in this capacity is active in Oxford's musical life as organist and conductor. His current research projects include issues in late nineteenth-century performance practice and analytical approaches to the later works of Wagner and Bruckner. He is a member of the editorial board and a regular contributor to 'The Wagner Journal'.

MARC ROCHESTER (b. 1954)
(S. Chad's 1984 – 1985)

Marc Rochester grew up in London where he was a chorister, and eventually had had organ lessons from Martin Neary at Westminster Abbey. He read music at the University of Wales (Cardiff), graduating with a B Mus degree. During this time he was Organ Scholar of Llandaff Cathedral under Robert Joyce. He was Assistant Organist of Bangor Cathedral from 1979-1981 and, at the age of 24, being one of the youngest people ever to be appointed to such a post in a British cathedral, he was Organist and Master of the Choristers of S. Columb's Cathedral, Londonderry from 1981-1982.

After his tenure of office at S. Chad's, Marc returned to Cardiff to complete his Doctorate and embarked upon a career in musical journalism, first as an arts correspondent and subsequently as a BBC presenter of arts programmes. He has long been associated with The Gramophone magazine and he has written for most of the leading musical magazines, dictionaries and encyclopaedias on music. In the late 1980s he was invited by the Government of Sarawak to work with the ethnic musicians of Borneo and produce the first commercial recording of their music.

Marc moved to Malaysia permanently and became lecturer at the country's first university music department. As well as being organist and programme annotator for the Malaysian Philharmonic Orchestra, he is also a resident writer of programme notes for such groups as the Hong Kong Philharmonic Orchestra, the Singapore Symphony Orchestra and the BBC Proms. He writes CD liner notes for Hyperion and Guild and writes for the Organists' Review. His book 'Putting Music into Words' was prompted by his work as an examiner for both the Associated Board of the Royal Schools of Music and Trinity Guildhall.

Since 1998 Marc has been the resident organist of Dewan Filharmonic Petronas (the twin towers) in Kuala Lumpur, where he gives regular recitals.

WILLIAM GEORGE SMALLMAN (b. 4 September 1941)
(S. Chad's 1985 – 2006)

Bill Smallman grew up in Bridgnorth where he had organ lessons from William Wood at S. Leonard's Church and attended Bridgnorth Grammar School. As a teenager he was Organist of Tasley Parish Church before going to study at the then Birmingham School of Music with George Miles where he received the GBSM diploma as well as an ARCO.

After graduation, Bill Smallman taught at the then Harlescott Grange Boys' Modern School in Shrewsbury. He was appointed Organist and Choirmaster of All Saints', Wellington in 1963, and where, for many years, he also taught at Dothill County Junior School. He remained at All Saints' for twenty two years before coming to S. Chad's as Director of Music in the autumn of 1985. He was the first person to hold the title 'Director of Music' which reflected the increasing complexity of the role, the appointee being responsible for overseeing all the church's music and not just the organ and the choir. In practice this had been the case for probably twenty years, but it is significant that now there was recognition of this in the title. Changes to the liturgical pattern and the subsequent changes to the musical life of S. Chad's have been documented elsewhere, as well as mention of the many concerts hosted by S. Chad's. Bill Smallman has been active in the musical life of the area as conductor of such groups as The County Singers as well as running the Country Choirs who sang an annual Evensong at Lichfield Cathedral for many years. Like many of his predecessors he has been President of The Shrewsbury and District Organists' and Choirmasters' Association on a number of occasions. He retired from S. Chad's on his 65th birthday in 2006, but remains active as an organist deputising at a number of churches throughout the county. He also retains a link with S. Chad's in so much that S. Mary's, now redundant, is part of the parish of S. Chad's and Bill is the curator of the fine four-manual Binns organ in S. Mary's.

After retirement from full-time teaching, and before retirement from S. Chad's, Bill started a series of Friday lunchtime organ recitals in the summer. These were the embryo of the present 'Concert in the Round' series which now runs each week for most of the year.

SUSAN CAROLINE HEATH-DOWNEY (b. 29 January 1954)
(S. Chad's for a short period in Autumn 2006)

Sue Heath Downey, originally from Devizes, studied at Queen Anne's School, Caversham, Reading, where she studied piano with Ruth Ascher and organ with Ewart Masser, Organist of Reading Town Hall. She subsequently studied organ, choir training, piano and harpsichord at The Royal Academy of Music, and as a post-graduate she studied with the late Nicholas Danby (on an Arts Council Scholarship), and with the late David Sanger. As well as the Graduate Diploma of the Royal Schools of Music (GRSM), she also obtained the LRAM, ARCM and ARCO diplomas. Three years were then spent working in sound recording for Argo/Decca where she worked on recordings with, amongst many top artists - Neville Marriner and the Academy of S. Martin in the Fields, the Phillip Jones Brass Ensemble, George Guest and the Choir of S. John's College, Cambridge, organist Peter Hurford and the Aeolian String Quartet. Sue then embarked upon a London-based freelance musical career working in many different musical fields including Stage Manager for Divertimento String Orchestra, reviewer for Classical Music Magazine, rehearsal pianist for S. Alban's Choral Society and for eighteen years as Artistic Director of the London Organ Days, an international event supported by the IAO.

Sue has had a glittering career as organist, harpsichordist, conductor and tutor, and as an organist has given recitals throughout the UK as well as in Australia, France, Germany, Italy, Norway and the USA. She was Organist & Director of Music at S. Magnus the Martyr, London Bridge for a number of years, having previously held posts at S. Paul's Shadwell and The German Church, Knightsbridge. Since 1998 she has been Founder-Conductor of the Rotherhithe and Bermondsey Choral Society, founding in 2009 the RBCS Chamber Orchestra. She is also Conductor of the Elizabethan Singers of London. Sue's tenure of office at S. Chad's was short owing to a serious illness, from which she made a full recovery. Since 2010 she has been Organist & Director of Music at S. Paul's Deptford.

DAVID LEEKE, (b. 10 May 1957)
(S. Chad's 2006 –)

David Leeke was born in Shrewsbury the son of George Leeke and Connie (née Edwards). He was a chorister at S. Chad's receiving his earliest lessons from Reg Harwood and later from Sam Baker, before continuing his studies at the Royal College of Music with John Birch (Organist of Chichester Cathedral), Robert Ashfield (Organist of Rochester Cathedral) and Peter Element. He also had some lessons there with Herbert Howells. During this time he was Assistant Organist of Croydon Parish Church (now Croydon Minster) under Michael Fleming, and lived at the RSCM Headquarters at Addington Palace, Croydon. In 1979 he moved to Folkestone to be Organist and Master of the Music at Folkestone Parish Church where he maintained the church's cathedral-like tradition. In Kent he taught at S. Augustine's College, Westgate-on-Sea before becoming Director of Music at S. Mary's College, Folkestone in 1987, during which time he was responsible for the installation of a new organ in the College Chapel.

He moved from Folkestone in 1990 to become Director of Music at Maidstone Grammar School (Britain's largest grammar school) where for ten years he ran an active music department. During this time he also held organists posts at S. Mary's, Kemsing and Christ Church, S. Leonard's-on-Sea. In addition to his full-time work, he was also Conductor of the East Malling Singers, Maidstone Operatic Society, Folkestone Symphony Orchestra and Tenterden Choral Society, as well as being the organ tutor for the Kent Centre for Young Instrumentalists (a specialist county-based school for talented young musicians).

David was for almost 25 years associated with the RSCM in Kent and North West Europe, being RSCM Chairman for Canterbury for many of them. For ten years he was Canterbury Diocesan Music Adviser where he was able to visit most of the 300 churches in the diocese and comment and advise on their diverse musical traditions. This post also afforded him the opportunity to conduct many diocesan occasions in Canterbury Cathedral, some of which were televised, and to have an input into the music at the 1998 Lambeth Conference. In 1996 he also became an examiner for the Associated Board of the Royal Schools of Music, being appointed to the training and moderating panel in 2001. In this capacity he has travelled extensively throughout the world, both on solo and group examining tours.

When David first returned to Shrewsbury, he was a for a time Master of the Music at Shrewsbury Abbey, before taking over at S. Chad's from Sue Heath-Downey at short notice in late autumn 2006. He has also been Conductor of Shrewsbury Cantata Choir since 2006.

At S. Chad's he has reinvigorated the musical life of the church and initiated a number of innovations. In addition to the post as held by his predecessors, he is also Artistic Director of S. Chad's Festival, Director of the Sam Baker Trust, and, following general staff restructuring at S. Chad's, has, since 2012 been Director of Music and Liturgy.

Part 3 – APPENDICES

Appendix 1

S. CHAD'S ORGANS

The first organ was in 1794 built by Robert and William Gray at a cost of 400 guineas which included a console and couplers as below:

Great (compass low GG to high f (58 notes)
Open Diapason 8
Stop Diapason 8
Principal 4
Twelfth 2 2/3
Fifteenth 2
Sesquialtera III
Mixture II
Trumpet 8
Cornet IV

Swell (compass as GT)
Open Diapason 8
Stop Diapason 8
Principal 4
Trumpet 8
Hautboy 8

Choir
Stopped Diapason 8
Flute [Probably 4]

Choir bass on swell keys below tenor F

1823
Pedals seem to have been added in c.1823 – presumably one stop.

1848
Organ cleaned and overhauled [and enlarged]

1861
Gray and Davison
New organ financed by Col Wingfield built by Gray and Davison [probably rebuild]

Console
Couplers
Swell to Great
Great to Pedal
Choir to Pedal

Pedal (Compass CCC – E (29 notes)
Open Diapason 16 [probably wood]

Great (compass CC – f (54 notes))
Open Diapason 8
Open Diapason 8 (TC replaced Mixture II)
Stopped Diapason 8
Clarabella 8 (replaced Cornet IV)
Principal 4
Twelfth 2 2/3
Fifteenth 2
Sesquialtera III
Trumpet 8

Swell (compass as Gt)
Double Diapason 16
Open Diapason 8
Stopped Diapason 8
Principal 4
Fifteenth 2
Sesquialtera III
Cornopean 8
Hautboy 8
Clarion 4

Choir (compass as Gt)
Bourdon 16 (CCC-BB 12 pipes)

Stopped Diapason Treble 8
Stopped Diapason Bass 8
Keraulophon 8
Dulciana 8
Principal 4
Flute 4
Cremona 8

3 composition pedals to great
2 composition pedals to swell

1883
cleaned by Gray & Davison

1904
N&B, Norwich
New organ –cost £1,550

Console

Couplers
Swell to Great
Swell to Pedal
Swell to Choir
Swell Octave
Great to Pedal
Choir to Great
Choir to Pedal

Pedal (compass CCC-f 30 notes)
Open Diapason 16 (wood)
Violone 16 (Gt Double)
Bourdon 16
Principal 8 (from Open Wood [called Octave]
Bass Flute 8
Trombone 16

Great (compass CC- a 58 notes)
Double Open Diapason 16

Large Open Diapason 8
Small Open Diapason 8
Hohl Flute 8
Corno Flute 8 [named Dolce]
Principal 4
Harmonic Flute 4
Fifteenth 2
Dulciana Mixture III
Tromba 8

Swell (compass as Gt)
Bourdon 16
Open Diapason 8
Stopped Diapason 8
Echo Gamba 8
Voix Celeste 8 (TC)
Principal 4
Wald Flute 4
Mixture III
Contra Fagotto 16
Horn 8 [called Cornopean]
Oboe 8
Vox Humana 8
Clarion 4
Tremulant

Choir (enclosed) (compass as Gt)
Lieblich Gedact 8
Violoncello 8
Dulciana 8
Lieblich Flute 4
Piccolo 2
Clarinet 8
Orchestral Oboe 8
Tremulant

Electric blowing
4 thumb pistons each to Great and Swell
2.4.4. composition pedals
Toe pedal for Gt to Ped

1963
Nicholson & Co
rebuild
Pedal (compass CCC-g 32 notes)
Open Diapason 16 (N&B wood)
Violone 16 (N&B; Great Double)
Bourdon 16 (N&B)
Quint 10 2/3 (N&B)
Principal 8 (N&B; from Open Diapason 16)
Bass Flute 8 (N&B; from Bourdon 16)
Flute 4 (Nicholson)
Trombone 16 (N&B)
Swell to Pedal
Swell Octave to Pedal
Great to Pedal
Choir to Pedal
Great to Pedal Pistons

Great (compass CC-a 58 notes)
Double Open Diapason 16 (N&B)
Large Open Diapason 8 (N&B)
Small Open Diapason 8 (N&B)
Hohl Flute 8 (N&B)
Principal 4 (N&B)
Harmonic Flute 4 (N&B)
Twelfth 2 2/3 (Nicholson; remade from Dolce)
Fifteenth 2 (N&B)
Mixture III (15-19-22) (N&B, remade, Nicholson)
Tromba 8 (N&B)
Swell to Great
Choir to Great

Swell (compass as Gt)
Bourdon 16 (N&B)
Open Diapason 8 (N&B)
Stopped Diapason 8 (N&B)
Echo Gamba 8 (N&B)
Viox Celeste 8 (TC) (N&B)
Viol d' Orchestre (N&B – a
sometime replacement for
the Vox Humana)
Principal 4 (N&B)
Wald Flute 4 (N&B)
Mixture III (15-19-22)
(N&B)
Contra Fagotto 16 (N&B)
Cornopean 8 (N&B)
Oboe 8 (N&B)
Clarion 4 (N&B)
Tremulant
Octave
Sub Octave
Unison Off

Choir (enclosed) (compass
as Gt)
Violoncello 8 (N&B)
Lieblich Gedact 8 (N&B)
Dulciana 8 (N&B)
Lieblich Flute 4 (N&B)
Gemshorn 4 (Nicholson)
Nazard 2 2/3 (Nicholson)
Piccolo 2 (N&B)
Clarinet 8 (N&B)
Tremulant
Octave
Sub Octave
Swell to Choir

Blowing electric
Accessories
6 adjustable thumb pistons
each to Great and Swell; 4 to
Choir;

6 adjustable toe pistons to
Great and Pedal;
reversible thumb pistons Sw-
Ped, Gt-Ped, Ch-Ped, Sw-Gt,
Gt Tromba;
reversible toe pistons Sw-Gt,
Gt-Ped, Ped Trombone;

1984
Harrison and Harrison
Adjustments made included
transposing the Choir
Gemshorn into a Tierce
1 3/5; replacing the Pedal
Principal with a metal stop
(from the Violone) of the
same name and the Pedal 4
foot Flute with a metal stop
(from the Violone called
Fifteenth.

1990
Harrison and Harrison
The Great Mixture was
remodelled and made into
(19-22-26) (in memory of the
parents of William Smallman,
then Director of Music)

2011
Harrison and Harrison
The organ underwent
a complete rebuild and
restoration with some tonal
adjustments and additions.
The action was completely
replaced and several new
playing aids were added.

Pedal (compass CCC-g 32
notes)
Resultant Bass 32 (N&B

former Nicholson Quint
2011)
Open Diapason 16 (N&B
wood)
Violone 16 (N&B; Great
Double)
Bourdon 16 (N&B)
Principal 8 (N&B; from Open
Diapason 16)
Bass Flute 8 (N&B; from
Bourdon 16)
Fifteenth 4 (N&B and H&H)
Trombone 16 (N&B)
Swell to Pedal
Swell Octave to Pedal
Great to Pedal
Choir to Pedal
Great to Pedal Pistons

Great (compass CC-a 58
notes)
Double Open Diapason 16
(N&B)
Large Open Diapason 8
(N&B)
Small Open Diapason 8
(N&B)
Hohl Flute 8 (N&B)
Principal 4 (N&B)
Harmonic Flute 4 (N&B)
Twelfth 2 2/3 (Nicholson;
remade from Dolce)
Fifteenth 2 (N&B)
Mixture III (15-19-22)
(N&B, remade, Nicholson &
remodelled H&H 1990)
Tromba 8 (N&B)
Swell to Great
Choir to Great
Swell (compass as Gt)
Bourdon 16 (N&B)
Open Diapason 8 (N&B)

Stopped Diapason 8 (N&B)
Echo Gamba 8 (N&B)
Viox Celeste 8 (TC) (N&B)
Principal 4 (N&B)
Wald Flute 4 (N&B)
Flageolet 2 (H&H 2011)
Mixture III (15-19-22)
(N&B) (remodelled H&H
2011)
Contra Fagotto 16 (N&B)
Cornopean 8 (N&B)
Oboe 8 (N&B)
Clarion 4 (N&B)
Tremulant
Octave
Sub Octave
Unison Off

Choir (enclosed) (compass
as Gt)
Violoncello 8 (N&B)
Violoncello Celestes 8
(former Swell Viol d'
Orchestre)
Lieblich Gedact 8 (N&B)
Lieblich Flute 4 (N&B)
Nazard 2 2/3 (Nicholson)
Piccolo 2 (N&B)
Tierce 1.3/5 (Nicholson
Gemshorn remade H&H
1985)
Clarinet 8 (N&B)
Tuba 8 (unenclosed) (H&H
2011)
Tremulant

Octave
Sub Octave
Unison Off
Swell to Choir
Great to Choir

Blowing electric
Accessories
6 adjustable thumb pistons
each to Great, Swell and
Choir;
6 adjustable toe pistons to
Great and Pedal;
reversible thumb pistons Sw-
Ped, Gt-Ped, Ch-Ped, Sw-Gt,
Ped Trombone;
reversible toe pistons Sw-Gt,
Gt-Ped,
6 General Pistons affecting
the whole organ
Stepper + and – system

Appendix 2

A SELECTION OF CONCERT PROGRAMMES

Organ Recital by Richard Lloyd (Hereford Cathedral) – Saturday 6 May 1972

Prelude in C minor	J S Bach
Two Chorale Preludes	
Schmücke dich	J S Bach
Uns ist geboren ein kenderlein	Flor Peeters
Concerto in B flat	William Felton
Suite Medievale	Langlais
Entrée; Offertoire; Elevation; Communion; Acclamations	
Prelude and A Fancy	William Harris
Choral in A minor	Cesar Franck

The Liverpool Sandon Orchestra – Saturday 3 June 1972

Arrival of the Queen of Sheba	Handel
Romance in C (op 2)	Sibelius
Concerto no 4 for Horn K459	Mozart
Soloist: Julian Baker (Sam Baker's son)	
Divertimento in F	Mozart
Symphony 22 (The Philosopher)	Haydn

Organ Recital by Martindale Sidwell (S. Clement Danes and Hampstead Parish Church) – Saturday 17 June 1972

Partita 'Jesu, meine Freude'	Walther
From the Eighteen Chorale Preludes	J S Bach
Schmücke dich, O liebe Seele	
Herr Jesu, Christ, dich zu uns wend	
Prelude and Fugue in A minor	J S Bach
Claire de Lune	Vierne
Toccata and Fugue in D minor and major	Reger
Sketch in D flat	Schumann
Te Deum	Langlais

Organ Recital by David Boarder (S, Mary's, Shrewsbury and Director of Music, The Priory Boys' Grammar School, Shrewsbury) – Tuesday 15 August 1972

Concerto in A minor (1st movement)	Vivaldi/Bach
Toccata, Adagio and Fugue in C	J S Bach
Fugue à la Gigue	J S Bach
Seven Last Words from the Cross	Alan Ridout

Noel (no. 10)	Daquin
Prelude, Fugue and Variation	Cesar Franck
Impromptu	Vierne
Fantasie in E flat	Saint Saens
Toccata (Symphonie V)	Widor

Organ Recital by Sam Baker (S. Chad's, Shrewsbury) – Friday 18 August 1972

Overture to Athalia	Handel
Organ Concerto in F (The Cuckoo and the Nightingale)	Handel
Introduction and Toccata	William Walond
Dorian Toccata and Fugue in D minor	J S Bach
Scherzo in G minor	Bossi
Pazienza	Whitlock
Toccatina for the flutes	Pietro Yon
Choral in A minor	Cesar Franck

Shrewsbury Chamber Singers and Orchestra – Friday 18 August 1972

Te Deum in C	Haydn
Vesperae Solemnes de Confessore	Mozart
Mass in G	Schubert

Organ Recital by Dr Caleb Jarvis (S. Andrew's, West Kirby and City Organist of Liverpool) – Saturday 19 August 1972

Toccata from Suite (op 14)	Maleingreau
Song of Sunshine	Hollins
Sonata 18 in A major	Rheinberger
Grave; Cappricio; Iddyle, Finale	
Sarabande	Caleb Jarvis
Variations on 'Weinen, Klagen, Sorgen, Zagen'	Liszt

Organ Recital by Sam Baker at Lichfield Cathedral (one of the opening recitals on the newly restored organ) – Sunday 4 August, 1974

Voluntary in C minor	Greene
Overture to Athalia	Handel
Introduction and Toccata	Walond
Chorale Prelude: Schmücke dich, O liebe, Seele	J S Bach
Fugue in E flat (S. Anne)	J S Bach
Introduction and Passacaglia (Sonata 8)	Rheinberger
Pazienza	Whitlock
Choral in A minor	Franck

Organ Recital by Sam Baker (S. Chad's) – Friday 15 August 1975

Overture to Athalia	Handel
Organ Concerto in F (The Cuckoo and the Nightingale)	Handel
Voluntary in D minor	Walond
Prelude on 'Rhosymedre'	Vaughan Williams
First of Three Impressions	Karg Elert
Introduction and Passacaglia	Alcock

Organ Recital by David Leeke (pupil of Sam Baker at S. Chad's) – Saturday 16 August 1975

Arrival of the Queen of Sheba	Handel
Chorale Prelude: Christ unzer Herr zum Jordan kam	J S Bach
Andante Tranquillo (Five Short Pieces)	Whitlock
Tuba Tune in D	Lang
Sketch in D flat	Schumann
Chorale Prelude on 'Rockingham'	Parry
Sonata No 2 in C minor	Mendelssohn

Grave; Adagio; Allegro maestoso e Vivace

(NB…there is no mention of the Fugue which completes this Sonata)

Organ Recital by Richard Pilliner (Royal Academy of Music student) – Friday 10 August 1979

Fantasia and Fugue in G minor (BWV 542)	J S Bach
Trio Sonata no 6 in G major (BWV 530)	J S Bach
Claire de Lune	Vierne
Toccata	Jongen

Organ Recital by Roy Woodhams (S. John's, Margate) – Friday 10 August 1979

Prelude and Fugue in C minor	Mendelssohn
Prelude on 'Rhosymedre'	Vaughan Williams
Prelude and Fugue in D major	J S Bach
Psalm Prelude (Set 1, no 2)	Howells
Sonata in G (first movement)	Elgar
Toccatina for the flutes	Yon
Prelude, Fugue and Variation	Franck
Te Deum	Langlais

Organ Recital by Peter Newell (S. Andrew's, Croydon) – Saturday 11 August 1979

Prelude and Fugue in A minor	J S Bach
Trio Sonata no 4 in E minor	J S Bach
Prelude on 'Martyrdom'	Parry
Voluntary in A minor	Stanley

A Fantasy	Darke
Folk Tune	Whitlock
Choral no 2 in B minor	Franck

Organ Recital by Reginald Adams (Holy Trinity, Broadstairs) – Friday 10 August 1990

Three Chorale Preludes:	Parry
Dundee; Melcombe; S. Anne	
Psalm Prelude (Set 1 no 2)	Howells
Dusk	Armstrong Gibbs
Humereske	Alec Rowley
An Old Time Tune	Easthope Martin
Elegy	Thalben Ball
Postlude	Norman Gilbert
Carmelite Suite	Jean Francaix
Sister Blanche	
Mother Marie of the Incarnation	
Sister Anne of the Cross	
Sister Constance	
Sister Mathilde	
Mother Marie of S. Augustine	
Passefied	Delibes
Hungarian March	Berlioz

Organ Recital by Reginald Adams (Holy Trinity, Broadstairs) – Saturday 17 August 1991

Toccata in G; Chant Pastorale; Noel	Dubois
Fantasia and Fugue in D minor	Stanford
Fantasy Prelude	Ernest Farrar
Minuet in B minor	Gigout
Grand Choeur	Salomé
Pavane and Galliard	Philip Cranmer
Folk Tune	Whitlock
Postlude	Norman Gilbert

Orgna Recital by Reginald Adams (Holy Trinity, Broadstairs) – Friday 14 August 1992

Toccata and Choral no. 1	Andriessen
Cantilene Pastorale	Guilmant
Sonata 14 in C	Rheinberger
Prelude; Idyll; Toccata	
An Irish Souvenir	Reginald Redman
Folk Tune and Scherzo	Whitlock
Three Miniatures	Gordon Phillips
Marche Pontificale	Widor

Organ Recital by Roy Woodhams (Director of Music, Ripon College, Cuddesdon) – Friday 14 August 1992

Prelude and Fugue in D	Buxtehude
Cornet Voluntary	Henry Heron
Elegy	Thalben Ball
Choral Variations on 'Veni Creator Spiritus'	Duruflé
Arabesque	Vierne
Litanies	Alain
Psalm Prelude (Set 1, no 1)	Howells
Aria	Flor Peeters
Toccata (Symphonie V)	Widor

S. Chad's Festival Chorus (conductor: David Leeke; organist: Roger Muttitt) – Saturday 15 August 1992

Comfort O Lord, the soul of thy servant	Crotch
If we believe that Jesus died and rose again	Goss
How beautiful upon the mountains	Stainer
Ave verum corpus	Elgar
O thou the central orb	Wood
God be merciful	David Grundy
Sing Choirs of Heaven	Shephard

Organ Recital by Roger Muttitt (Music Staff, Felsted School) – Saturday 15 August 1992

Music from the Royal Fireworks	Handel
Choral no 2 in B minor	Franck
Final from Symphonie VIII	Widor

Organ Recital by David Leeke (Director of Music, Maidstone Grammar School) in memory of Sam Baker – Monday 17 August 1992

Overture to Athalia	Handel
Choral Prelude: Christ unzer Herr zum Jordan kam	J S Bach
Rhapsody in D flat	Howells
'Nimrod' from Enigma Variations	Elgar
'Fidelis' (Four Extemporisations)	Whitlock
Introduction and Passacaglia	Alcock

Centenary Organ Recital by Jennifer Bate – Tuesday 15 February 2005

Fantasia and Toccata in D minor	Stanford
Eight Variations in B flat on 'God save the King'	Samuel Wesley
Fugue in E minor	Mendelssohn

Two Fragments by Mendelssohn and completed by Jennifer Bate:

Chorale and Variation in D minor

Allegro assai in C

INTERVAL

March on a Theme by Handel	Guilmant
Prelude and Fugue on the name ALAIN	Duruflé
Le jardin suspendu	Alain
Choral-Improvisation sur le 'Victimae Paschali laudes'	Tournemire
transcribed by Maurice Duruflé	

Organ Recital by David Leeke (part of the Friday lunchtime 'Concerts in the Round' series) – Friday 2 May 2008

Fanfare	Wills (b. 1926)
Chorale Prelude 'Heut Triumphiret Gottes Sohn	
J S Bach (1685-1750)	
Sarabande for the Morning of Easter	
Howells (1892-1983)	
Theme and Variations	Andriessen (1892-1981)
Folk Tune	Whitlock (1903-1946)
March on a Theme by Handel	Guilmant (1837-1911)

Organ Recital by Richard Walker (part of the Festival) – Sunday 3 May 2009

Prelude – The Spitfire	Walton (1902-1983)
Prelude and Fugue in C (BWV 547)	J S Bach (1685-1750)
Sonata no 5 in D	Mendelssohn (1809-1847)
Andante; Andante con moto; Allegro	
Naiades (Piéce de Fantasie, op 55)	Vierne (1870-1937)
Nocturne	Hollins (1865-1942)
Toccata (Suite, op 5)	Duruflé (1902-1986)

Flute Recital by Katherine Baker with Jonathan Baker, piano (part of the Festival) – Sunday 1 May 2011

Sonata for Flute and Piano	Poulenc (1899-1963)
Allegro malincolico; Cantelena: assez lent; Presto giocoso	
Syrinx	Debussy (1862-1918)
Violin Sonata no 3	Delius (1862-1934)
transcribed for flute by Tony Summers – world première	
Slow; Andante scherzando – meno mosso – Tempo primo;	
Lento – Con moto – Tranquillo – Tempo primo	
Nocturne et Allegro scherzando	Gaubert (1879-1941)

Inagural Recital after the 2011 organ rebuild by Roy Massey – Saturday 21 January 2012

Toccata in G	Théodore Dubois (1837-1924)
Four Polish Dances	Jan Z Lublina (16th century)
Poznania	
Rocal Fuza	
Eszcze Marczynye	
Hayduczky	
Toccata in F (BWV 540)	J. S. Bach (1685-1750)
Prelude, Fugue and Variation	César Franck (1822-1890)
Fantasy on	
Babylon's Streams	William Harris (1883-1973)
Will o' the Wisp	Gordon Balch Nevin (1892-1943)
Tuba Tune	Norman Cocker (1889-1953)
La Cinquantaine	Gabriel Marie (1852-1928)
(arr. William Carl)	
Toccata-Prelude on	
Vom Himmel Hoch	Garth Edmundson (1892-1971)

Organ Recital by Simon Preston – Saturday 28 January 2012

Prelude and Fugue in A minor (BWV 543)	J. S. Bach (1685-1750)
Fantasia in F minor/major (K594)	Mozart (1756-1791)
Les Anges and Dieu parmi nous	Messiaen (1908-1992)
(from La Nativité)	
Phantasie on 'Ad nos, ad salutarem'	Liszt (1811-1886)

Organ Recital by Richard Walker (Assistant Director of Music, S. Chad's) – Saturday 4 February 2012

Prelude – The Spitfire	Walton (1902 – 1983) arr Morrell
Academic Festival Overture	Brahms (1833 – 1897) arr Lemare
Sonata No 1 in Eb, BWV 525	J S Bach (1685 – 1750)
Allegro moderato, Adagio, Allegro	

Two pieces by Vierne (1870 – 1937)
Berceuse (from 24 pièces en style libre)
Naiades (from Pièces de Fantaisie, 4e suite)
Three pieces by Karg-Elert (1877 – 1933)
The Mirrored Moon,
(from Seven Pastels from the Lake of Constance, Op 96)
Choral Improvisation: Jerusalem, du hochgebaute Stadt,
Op 65, No 48
Valse mignonne, Op 142, No 3

The Chrysanthemum – an Afro-American Intermezzo	Scott Joplin (1867 – 1917) arr E Power Biggs
Toccata di Concerto, Op 59	Lemare (1866 – 1934)

Organ Recital by David Leeke (in memory of his mother, Connie Leeke, 1924-2011) – Saturday 11 February 2012

Trumpet Voluntary	Stanley (1712-1786)
Voluntary in C	Stanley
Adagio; Andante; Slow; Allegro	
Chorale Prelude, BWV 684	J S Bach (1685 – 1750)
Christ unzer Herr zum Jordan kam	
Two Preludes on Hymn Tunes:	
Rockingham	Parry (1848-1918)
Down Ampney	Ley (1887-1962)
Two pieces connected with Connie:	
The White Cliffs of Dover	
Londonderry Air	Stanford (1852-1924)
Two organ arrangements of music by Edward Elgar (1857-1934)	
Nimrod	
The Angel's Farewell (Gerontius)	
Grand Choeur	Guilmant (1837-1911)

Appendix 3

SHROPSHIRE MUSIC TRUST CONCERTS

Thursday 18 October 1984	Vlado Perlemuter (piano)
Friday 16 November 1984	London Baroque
Friday 8 February 1985	The Medici String Quartet
Friday 22 March 1985	The Midland Boy Singers
Tuesday 12 December 2000	Ex Cathedra: Christmas by Candlelight
Monday 10 December 2001	Ex Cathedra: Christmas by Candlelight
Friday 6 December 2002	Ex Cathedra: Christmas by Candlelight
Tuesday 9 December 2003	Ex Cathedra: Christmas by Candlelight
Thursday 4 November 2004	The London Mozart Players with Emma Johnson, (clarinet)
Tuesday 7 December 2004	Ex Cathedra: Christmas by Candlelight
Tuesday 3 May 2005	Ex Cathedra: At the foot of the Cross
Tuesday 22 November 2005	James Kirby (piano)
Tuesday 6 December 2005	Ex Cathedra: Christmas by Candlelight
Thursday 2 February 2006	City of London Sinfonia conducted by Nicholas Ward
Tuesday 4 December 2007	Ex Cathedra: Christmas by Candlelight
December 2006	Ex Cathedra: Christmas by Candlelight
Thursday 10 April 2008	The Sixteen: Treasures of Tudor England (part of The Sixteen's Choral Pilgrimage) conducted by Harry Christophers
Sunday 26 October 2008	Black Dyke Mills Band conducted by Nicolas Childes
Monday 24 November 2008	Manchester Camerata conducted by Douglas Boyd, with John Lill (piano)
Thursday 11 December 2008	Ex Cathedra: Christmas by Candlelight
Saturday 2 May 2009	Black Voices (part of the annual S. Chad's Festival)
Tuesday 27 October 2009	English Chamber Orchestra conducted by Paul Watkins with William Bennett (flute)
Tuesday 15 December 2009	Ex Cathedra: Christmas by Candlelight
Thursday 3 June 2010	The Sixteen: Treasures of Renaissance England (part of The Sixteen's Choral Pilgrimage) conducted by Harry Christophers
Tuesday 7 December 2010	Ex Cathedra: Christmas by Candlelight
Friday 18 February 2011	Scottish Ensemble with Alison Balsom, (trumpet)
Tuesday 7 June 2011	John Williams and John Etheridge (guitars)

A SELECTION OF SOME OF THE LITURGICAL MUSIC SUNG BY THE ADULT CHOIR 2007 – 2012

This is a selection of repertoire taken from music lists for the Sunday Services:

EUCHARIST SETTINGS

Lennox Berkeley	Missa Brevis
William Byrd	Mass for Four Voices
Anthony Caesar	Missa Brevis Capella Regalis
Bob Chilcott	A Little Jazz Mass
Haydn	The Little Organ Mass
Martin How	The Shrewsbury Mass
Christopher Mabley	Missa Brevis
Mozart	Missa Brevis in D
Palestrina	Missa Brevis
Adrian Williams	S. Chad's Mass

EVENSONG CANTICLES

Brewer	in D
Dyson	in D
Gibbons	The Short Service
Harris	in A
Harwood	in A flat
Holman	in F minor
Hylton Stewart	in C
Richard Lloyd	The Shrewsbury Service
Moeran	in D
Sumsion	in G
Murrill	in E
Nicholson	in D flat
Noble	in B minor
Purcell	in G minor
Stanford	in B flat
Stanford	in C

EVENSONG RESPONSES

Ayleward
Ebdon
Evans
Leeke
Reading
Rose
Sanders
William Smith

Stanford	in G
Sumsion	in G
Walmisley	in D minor
Watson	in E
Weelkes	for trebles

ANTHEMS

Albert (Prince Consort)	Jubilate
Allegri	Misere mei
Malcolm Archer	Various pieces
Peter Aston	So they gave their bodies
Peter Aston	The true glory
Bainton	And I saw a new heaven
Bairstow	Blessed City
Bairstow	Jesu, the very thought
Bairstow	Let all mortal flesh
Bairstow	The Lamentations
Sam Baker	Ave Maria
Berkeley	Look up, sweet babe
Frederick Bridge	Happy is the man that findeth wisdom (written for the funeral of Charles Darwin)
Bruckner	Locus iste
Bull	In the departure of the Lord
Bullock	Give us the wings of faith
Byrd	Ave verum
Byrd	Sacerdotes Domini
Chilcott	Be thou my vision
Cornelius	Three Kings
Crotch	Lo star-led chiefs
Duruflé	Ubi caritas
Eccard	When to the temple
Elgar	Ave verum corpus
Elgar	Light of the world
Brian Evans	God be in my head
Finzi	God is gone up
Michael Fleming	Kindle a light
Gardiner	Evening Hymn

Gibbons	Almighty and everlasting God
Gibbons	This is the record of John
Greene	Thou visitest the earth
Grieg	Ave Maris stella
David Grundy	God be merciful
Guest	For the fallen
Handel	Hallelujah
Handel	Since by man came death
Harris	Behold the tabernacle
Harris	Holy is the true light
Haydn	Insanae et vanae curae
Haydn	The heavens are telling
Hilton	Lord, for thy tender mercy's sake
Holst	Turn back O man
Howells	A spotless Rose
Ireland	Greater Love
Ives	Listen sweet Dove
John of Portugal	Crux Fidelis
Lauridsen	O magnim mysterium
David Leeke	A New Commandment
Simon Lole	Father of all, when we were still far off
Simon Lole	The Journey
Loosemore	O Lord, Increase my faith
Richard Lloyd	From glory to glory
Richard Lloyd	View me Lord
Mendelssohn	Above all praise and majesty
Mendelssohn	He that shall endure to the end
Mendelssohn	Hear my prayer
Mendelssohn	Lift thine eyes
Morley	Nolo mortem peccatoris
Mozart	Ave verum corpus
Mozart	Laudate Dominum
Ord	Adam lay ybounden
Parry	Crossing the bar
Parry	I was glad

Parry	My soul there is a country
Pergolesi	Stabat Mater
Poulenc	Litanies à la Vierge Noire
Poulenc	O magnum mysterium
Purcell	Thou knowest, Lord
Rutter	God be in my head
Rutter	The Lord bless you
Sanders	The Reproaches
Schutz	Praise to thee, Lord Jesus
Shephard	Sing Choirs of Heaven
Stainer	God so loved the world
Stainer	I saw the Lord
Stanford	Beati quorum
Stanford	Justorum animae
Stanford	Ye Choirs of New Jerusalem
Tallis	If ye love me
Tavener	Song for Athene
Tchaikovsky	Hymn to the Trinity
Tye	Laudate nomen Domini
Vaughan Williams	Rise Heart (Five Mystical Songs)
Vaughan Williams	O clap your hands
Vaughan Williams	O taste and see
Victoria	Popule meus
Victoria	O quam gloriosum
Granville Walker	I saw eternity
Warlock	Bethlehem Down
Warlock	Benedicamus Domino
Wesley	Ascribe unto the Lord
Wesley	Blessed be the God and Father
Wesley	Wash me throughly
Wesley	Thou wilt keep him
Whitacre	The Marriage
Whitlock	Here, O my Lord
Adrian Williams	Hail Mary

A SELECTION OF SOME OF THE PERFORMERS IN THE CONCERTS IN THE ROUND SERIES 2007 – 2012

Anne Tupling (violin)
Arcadi Ensemble
Baroquenroll (chamber ensemble)
Barrie Mackay and Richard Walker (piano duets)
Border Voices
Carol Shippey (soprano)
Carolyn Chadwick (soprano)
Colla Voce (vocal quartet)
Corinne Frost (cello)
Counterpoint (chamber ensemble)
Emma Boger (soprano)
Emma Lindsay (flute)
David Joyce (violin)
David Lewis (baritone)
Florentine Wind Quintet
Gay Walker (horn)
Helen Schilsky (viola)
Helen Wearing (viola)
Hollie Whittles (clarinet)
James Gower (bass)
Jamie Brownfield Jazztet
Jennie Bianco (soprano)
John Bowen (baritone)
Julian Hartmann (piano)
Laura Collins (vocal-led jazz)
Lauren Hibberd (piano)
Louise Salmond-Smith (recorder)
Madeleine Ridd (cello)
Marek Orszulik (guitar)
Michael Arthur (baritone)
Michael Broadway (pianola)

Michael Sheehan (horn)
Nick Curror (piano)
Paul Mocroft (baritone)
Pupils from Birmingham Conservatoire
Pupils from Chetham's School of Music, Manchester
Pupils from Concord College
Pupils from Newport Girls' High School
Pupils from Shrewsbury School
Pupils from Shrewsbury International School, Bangkok
Pupils from Shrewsbury High School
Richard Silk (piano/ harpsichord)
Robin Ward (harp)
Robson Piano Duo
Sarah Westwood (soprano)
Shropshire Wind Ensemble
Simon Dearsley (piano)
Stella Seaton-Sims (mezzo soprano)
Sterling Trio
Students from Shrewsbury College
Susie Allen (piano)
Tim Kennedy (tenor)
Trio Preti
Wendy Jones (trumpet)

Organ Recitalists:

Ian Curror
Nicholas Danks
Peter Dyke
Andrew Earis
David Flood
John Godwin
Peter Gould
Ian Hare
William Hayward
Carl Jackson
Theo Jones
Cathy Lamb
David Leeke
Simon Lole
Tim Mills
Robert Munns
Francis Murton
Timothy Noon
Daniel Phillips
David Price
Nigel Pursey
William Smallman
Christopher Symons
Allan Walker
Richard Walker
Shaun Ward
John Wardle
Roy Woodhams